Be the Parent, Not the Pal

HIGH GEAR PARENTING TIPS IN A CRAZY, DIGITAL WORLD

Amy Donaho Howell

© 2018 Amy Donaho Howell
All rights reserved.

ISBN: 1983568759
ISBN 13: 9781983568756

1

This book is dedicated to our children, Bryan and Abby and also to all of their friends who have enriched our lives, entertained us and supported our family. We love you all and are grateful for the mounds of joy you bring us. Thank you for being such good kids and embracing your value system which we hope will serve as your own GPS in your lives. We hope one day when you are parents yourselves, you will look back and remember and appreciate some of the things we taught you, gave you and inspired in you.

This book is also dedicated to all parents out there raising good kids in this crazy world. We hope you love our stories, tips and experiences. Parenting is the hardest, most important and most rewarding job ever!

Chapter Outline

Introduction ix

Chapter 1 Your Values: Your GPS in Life 1

Chapter 2 Foundational Years are Critical 11

Chapter 3 Smartphones: Good, Bad, Ugly 38

Chapter 4 The Opioid Epidemic, Teen Drinking and Tougher Issues 46

Chapter 5 7 Nights at the Dinner Table: The Decline of Family Activities 67

Chapter 6 Bullying, Peer Pressure & Jealousy 71

Chapter 7 Social Media 87

Chapter 8 Common Sense Isn't Common 93

Chapter 9 Schools: What are we REALLY Teaching our Children 99

Chapter 10 High Gear in College ································· 102

Chapter 11 Choices and Consequences ···························· 107

Chapter 12 Accountability ···································· 114

Chapter 13 Grandparents: Standing in the Gap ···················· 117

Conclusion If we had to do it all over again....
what would we do differently? ·························· 123

Introduction

I wanted to write and share this book because I think parenting is one of the hardest and most important jobs anyone can ever do. It requires much sacrifice, selflessness and patience. It requires so much stamina and endurance, and can be all consuming. And it requires parents to actually BE a parent, not a pal to our kids. I believe so many parents are worried about offending their kids or hurting their kids' feelings that they end up hurting their chances at success. Parents who think that their kids exist to become their best friends are actually not helping themselves or their kids. It seems like recently that so many parents view themselves as their kids' pals instead of the authoritative, mentoring, guiding adult they should be. And I'm not going to sugarcoat anything here in this book, so I hope you won't mind my "straight talk" style of telling it like it is from my viewpoint.

I wanted also to write and release this book during a time in American history where we, as a nation, are experiencing culture wars, rapidly advancing technology (social media platforms) and digital social awkwardness and decline of civility, to say the least. We live in a time when political correctness rules, which I also think is killing the spirit of traditional American values. Corruption--in Government, Corporate America, Hollywood, Education, Media--has run wild and unrestrained. Integrity is a word we rarely hear anymore but is foundational to success as a person. We need to teach our kids good manners and etiquette so that when they grow up, they will have class and will know that there is a time and a place for our words. Just because we can say something, doesn't mean we should.

Social media has given us "keyboard warriors" who spew hatred and mean-spirited content at each other daily. We have lost our ability to be kind and civil to one another if we disagree or have different viewpoints. We must teach our kids a better way to coexist and help create better ways to communicate with one another. Kindness is needed everywhere. We must all work on being kind to one another because I believe it really matters.

We work in a global economy where our kids will one day have to compete. Times have changed so radically in the past 50 years (during my lifetime) that I don't know how parents will be able to keep up in the next 50. I think our kids need all the help they can get and I worry that technology and social media will have long term, profound impacts on our kids. You don't have to look very far to see the increase in suicide rates, mental illness and teen drug and alcohol abuse. Our kids need us more now than ever.

In spite of everything I just said, parenting good kids in a crazy world is possible and attainable of course. In fact, I believe that we must strive to raise good kids in order that they can make some changes and hopefully inject some of the more traditional values back into our society. And by traditional values (maybe I should use the word "historical"), I mean things such as having civil conversations, listening to speakers who have differing views (not protesting in violence), getting out from behind a keyboard to have real life conversations, etc. **I believe there is a direct connection between**

raising good, responsible kids and our health and wealth as a society and nation. As parents, I think we need a call to action back to making sure we are bringing good future human beings into this world in which we all coexist. In short, we need to turn the ship around and sail it back to better, and more calm waters (maybe before we sink it).

I am not a PhD, an MD nor a psychologist. I am a 53+ year-old wife, mom, marketing consultant, author and dog owner who has somehow managed--with my husband as my teammate--to raise two pretty good kids. I have worked hard in the corporate world over the past 30 years, building what some might say is a successful career. I have hired employees, mentored them, and have given back to the community where I work and live. I have served on boards, volunteered, raised money and have met and worked with some incredible people along the way. I have loved my work, but let me tell you it was easier than raising kids. Raising kids is without a doubt harder than any job I have had--or ever will have--in the workforce. As our youngest, Abby, heads off to college, I am watching some interesting dynamics unfold in our world today.

It's not easy being a kid these days. While being a parent may be tough, being a kid is no picnic. If you think it was tough to be a kid back in our day (1970's) think about how hard it is now. Our kids are so bombarded with information and technology that I think we may need a time out at some point. I don't know what all of the answers are, but I think we need to ask the questions. When I see my kids--and all our kids--with their heads constantly in their phones, I wonder what it is doing to them and us. What is the "selfie" obsession doing to kids as they develop their self esteem? That's why I wanted to write this book. To help other parents who maybe are just getting started with families or maybe have kids about to hit the crossing over points: getting a smartphone and driving.

I hope you like this book. If you do, be sure to check out some of my other books co-authored by my friend and colleague Anne Deeter Gallaher. Together we wrote and published "Women in High Gear" and "Students in High Gear," both guides to attaining high gear goals in life, college and work. I also wrote one on sepsis survival, patient safety and advocacy titled "Healing in High Gear." All of these books are available on Amazon.

CHAPTER 1
Your Values: Your GPS in Life

"Children are not casual guests in our home. They have been loaned to us temporarily for the purpose of loving them and instilling a foundation of values on which their future lives will be built."
--JAMES DOBSON

Value: A person's principles or standards of behavior; one's judgment of what is important in life (dictionary).

Genetics and the value system that a child has and nurtures, are by far the two greatest things that will determine the kind of adult one becomes. We cannot help or change the genetic pool from which we are born into but we can channel what values we hold dear and the reasons why we do. Key values are essential to success. I believe that values are formed at an early age--even babies can begin to form their values by what they see, experience and learn.

If a child is born into a broken family where drug abuse, crime and mental illness prevail, it is likely that child will grow up with those values and repeated behavior patterns that accompany them. Many kids today are born into poverty where crime and drugs are the mainstay values. Parents are often absent, on drugs and have kids simply to receive welfare. In order to break the vicious cycle--at some point--it takes courage and discipline to reject those values and turn to other ones. A few make it out, but unfortunately, many do not. We need more mentoring and adults that care in the lives of children. If children are our future, we need to get them educated and trained so that they may be employed and hopefully have hope for a happy life that opportunity provides.

I'm writing this book not to address these types of family problems (I'm not an expert on crime and poverty) but to acknowledge them. I believe every child has the right to a happy life filled with love, security and better values. If only we could figure out how to break the cycle of crime, drugs and poverty which often go hand in hand.

I remember growing up my parents would always say when someone did or did not have a "value system." Values--I believe--were more discussed and worn like badges of honor back in the day. In high school, we had labels like "most likely to succeed" or "most popular" --values often placed on someone. Knowing what your parents' value system was--in my childhood--essential to staying out of trouble. My parents spanked me or punished me when I strayed away from their values. They also praised, supported and encouraged me when I demonstrated holding our family values near and dear.

I was taught from the onset to embrace my set of values and stick with them throughout my life--at all phases. Many of my values are faith-based as I grew up in the Presbyterian Church and spent much of my developmental time in sunday school, church, youth group and choir. My dad was the senior minister at our church so I was a "pk" (preacher's kid) for life (and yes, I was teased constantly about it). So we pretty much were at church when the doors opened. But those faith-based values I hold near and dear in my life. They have been the values that I cling to and tried to pass along to our children.

Aside from being in church a lot, I worked and had a job at age fifteen and those values applied at work as well. As my parents taught me their values, I rarely ever questioned them and still don't. Values don't bend. They are unyielding and not to be compromised ever. Right is right, wrong is wrong. There is no "sort of right" just like there is no "version of the truth." As parents we must fight society's push to bend the truth, compromise our values and sell out for all the wrong reasons.

Values are like your compass or GPS through life. Good ones will steer you well and keep you off a dead end path. Like drugs are a dead end path for example. More on that later.

As parents to young children, we must think about our "value system" as a family and our values as individuals. You teach your baby love when you hold him and sing to him. You teach her values when you read to her and talk to her. As their tiny brains are soaking it all up preparing them for life, your values and how you relay them matter and become like compounding interest in a bank--an investment in your child's character. It's important before even having a child to subscribe to a certain set of values. I believe that successful parenting is founded on key values, taught early and nurtured and discussed often.

A great way to get started parenting is to think early about what your family values are and discuss them. As much as I knew what my values really were, having a baby will challenge you to reflect on them--rely on them as well. Good parenting values include being consistent and staying true to them in the face of challenges. A simple example I can share with you is that when our first born, Bryan, was an infant, people would invite us to dinner and parties often. Many of those invitations we politely declined. It was important to us to adopt a routine of normal bedtime, consistency and low stress for our newborn. While many parents would tote their infant anywhere at late hours--we opted not to. It wasn't just routine we valued but also the underlying security we were giving our new baby that he was safe in his bed each night--a secure place he knew (free of noise and strangers). That security translates into love for your child and should trump a parent's love for a social life. When you have a baby, you must make sacrifices that you didn't have to make before. Selflessness is something you value as a new parent. You have a dependent who needs you and so you adapt and embrace this new status.

For me, values are the roadmap for everything that comes your way as a parent. A simple way to keep you and your child in check when the tough times come--and they do. Your values guide you to help you make the best decisions. It's your values that will pop up when your child says, "but Mom, everyone else got a bad grade too." My conditioned response (and my kids will tell you this is true) was always "I'm not worried about 'everyone else.' I'm worried about you." The value is discipline and doing the right things over and over which will eventually become natural. Like getting good at a sport, practicing and perfecting doing the right things become automatic. Additionally, if you value certain things, your kids will too. They will also know it and can sometimes guess what you are going to say before you say it.

What are some of your key values? Do you value love? Do you value time with family? Do you value money? If so, make sure you keep it in perspective and don't let money rule your life. Valuing money and material possessions is natural. We all want better things for our kids and families.

However, I also think valuing money can be a downfall and obstacle to raising kids.

As a working mom, I had a constant guilt trip going on in my head about working outside of the home while raising kids. It was important to our family finances that I worked and my husband, Jim, did as well. We were both on serious career tracks at the time our children came along. Somehow we managed to stay on those tracks and raise kids at the same time. That did require some changes however. I decided to quit the "corporate job" and start my own consulting practice which I did and worked out of my home (More on all of that in our book, "Women in High Gear"). I knew I needed more flexibility and time with our newborn son. It was a leap of faith but it worked and I still (22 years later) have my consulting practice.

Money is both a blessing and a curse. You must value it only for the right reasons and guard against putting it too high on the priority list. Good parents set good examples for their kids. If you value money more than other things, you are telling your kids that money is the most important thing. If you give your kids too much money, they won't learn to earn it. Sometimes parents (and grandparents) struggle with how much is too much. It can create problems in families.

I'll share a story of when I was a teenager that has had a lifetime impact on me and how I view money. One night when I was about 15 or 16, I was in my room and it was summer in Mobile, AL. Mobile is deep south in Alabama and not far from the Gulf of Mexico. It was hot and humid and--although we had air conditioning--my parents sometimes didn't turn it on. We lived on the income my Dad made as a minister and my awesome Mom did her best feeding, clothing and educating three girls on a tight budget. In 1978 that income was not much. On this hot night, I heard my parents talking about the air conditioning and the expense of turning it on. Luckily for me, I had a good job (2 actually: babysitting and lifeguarding) and had saved about $400 in cash. I had the cash in one of those old fashioned jewelry boxes that snapped shut and I kept it in my room. When I heard this discussion about air conditioning, I picked up that jewelry box, knocked on my parents' bedroom door and gave them the box of cash (I had more in my bank account). I told them that our family was a team and that I could help. I gave my Dad the cash and told them to run that air conditioner. A working girl needed her sleep! And I've been working ever since that hot, summer night.

Both of our kids had jobs as soon as they could drive and that teaches them the value of the dollar--you earn it. Parents who don't make or allow their kids to work (for pay)--in my opinion--are doing a great disservice to their futures. Working not only teaches kids the value of the dollar, but it teaches them life skills for later when they hopefully graduate from college. I also believe that kids who have jobs gain a jump in life on those who do not. They have a debit card and a bank account to manage (and they see how fast it can go). They have a boss who is not their parent and the added experience of working with co-workers is a great way to teach responsibility and other life skills.

Money--or the lack of--can be very destructive: I don't know which is worse: too much money or not enough. I think if I had to choose, I'd say not enough. Parents who have to struggle daily to put food on the table and buy clothes for kids are stressed out. And let's face it--many of us are. Food, clothing education--everything is getting more and more expensive. It is very expensive to have children, and I think it is getting even harder to balance things financially for many families.

As I write this, I saw a call for "parents to do better" on Facebook by spreading the idea not to make expensive gifts from "Santa" at Christmas.

The idea is that kids who don't have much get simple gifts from Santa (like food and blankets) while others get lavish gifts. One child asked his mom, "does Santa love them more than me?" It sure is something to think about and it struck me that we all need to remember that many kids have very little.

We have been mostly fortunate in this regard in that we seemed to have what we needed--working hard to have it. However, having said that, we have also recently experienced having a lot less and it is stressful. A job loss, a medical issue--anything can happen that puts one's earning potential at risk or on hold. Financial problems make parenting even more difficult. My best advice to young parents is to work as much as you can while you are young and **SAVE YOUR MONEY!** Start saving as soon as you can, and commit to the discipline of doing it. It may mean you have to sacrifice some things but do it anyway. Get a good banker and financial planner (those are not necessarily the same) who can help you map out your savings plan. You never know what the future holds and a good financial planner can help you prepare for what can happen later.

Here are some tips for raising kids on a good value system:

- Write down your family values and discuss them often
- Make the first value unconditional love for your family: what does it mean? Make sure you communicate it often
- Start early with your infants and think about the examples you set
- Stress the importance of telling the truth early; some of the worst trouble for my kids came if they didn't tell the truth--a foundational value in my opinion
- Make being kind and compassionate to others a value and show them--take meals to the sick; offer to help someone in need; demonstrate daily acts of kindness

- Paint your values on wooden signs and hang them in a bathroom or playroom (or buy them--they are everywhere these days--for a reason)
- Read inspiring books about values and get encouragement for standing by them
- Resist the urge to listen to what other parents say--think for yourself
- Pray for God's hand in parenting and ask Him to guide you
- Encourage and praise your kids when they exhibit your values: there is nothing more rewarding to me as when my child does something positive exhibiting core values

Some of our family values are love, respect, kindness, trust, freedom, honesty, courage and strength.

Creating this list made me think of another point that I think is important, especially for new parents. When you first have a baby, you may feel at a loss for what to do as you enter this new phase in your life. It's normal to feel like you have crossed over to some unknown territory (like swimming in the deep end when you first do it--right?). What you must NOT do is put too much stock into what other parents are saying if it goes against your gut feelings. I remember early on having conversations with parents with older kids that I had to get my baby on a waiting list for a certain school. I remember the pressure they put on me to do it. It raised a red flag and my inner voice told me something else. We ended up moving out of the city and to a rural area with a great public school system. We found a house we could afford on 4 acres with a lake where our kids and dogs could play and run (and I could breathe). And we bought it for less money than we sold our city house for. Not only did our kids go to school on a yellow school bus, but they went to a very diverse, public school with great teachers and I didn't have to get "on a list." They also can benefit by going to a public school where pampering and coddling is not allowed. Public schools are more like the real world and I have always been grateful for my own public school exposure.

The money we saved by putting them into public school enabled us to invest in other ways. Every family must do what is right for them. Our values were different than some of our friends' values. I'm not judging them for their choices, our choices were just different. We did not join private clubs nor did we participate in the many social offerings at them. Instead, we used our extra (and hard-earned) money to build a river house that we took our kids to often. We valued family time together and we love watersports so we took our young children to the river (actually it's the Tennessee River) where they learned to ski, wakeboard, surf and swim. We invited our friends and their kids and constantly had a boat full of kids. Those memories are documented in the 14 or so photo albums we have there. And it has become our family "gathering" spot. Hopefully, someday our kids will have their own children and make those same memories there.

Parents, if you have a good public school option near you, why not consider that and save a ton of money. Private schools--although excellent in many ways--are expensive. Maybe even consider delaying private schooling until later. We admittedly moved our youngest to a private middle school and high school after our public school system went through some transition that resulted in our decision. However, in doing the math, we paid for a river house by not doing private schools for two kids for the most part. At $15,000 (average) per year per child, that's a lot of money that could be invested.

Think about what is right for you and your family. Your kids will be just fine if they have to ride a bus or go to a public school. I believe good kids with strong values end up fine no matter what school they attend. Don't feel pressured to do what "everyone else" is doing and if your friends try and tell you that you are less of a parent for not conforming, get new friends! Take it from someone older (like me), none of that small stuff matters in the end.

CHAPTER 2

Foundational Years are Critical

"Adopt the pace of nature: her secret is patience"
--Ralph Waldo Emerson

Perhaps the most important characteristic of being a parent is having patience. The everlasting type. The type that gets you through many storms--calms you when you would like to have a nervous breakdown that you probably deserve. Patience is key to good parenting. We learn that without being patient, we'd set our kids up for failure. Kids are going to fail. We all do. We have to be patient with our kids--especially during puberty--and at each stage. So it is with a broad brush that I recommend painting patience across every aspect of parenting. It's fundamental to success, in my opinion--not only raising kids but in just about everything we do.

Although the early years of parenting are harder physically, they are somewhat easier than the pre-teen and teenage years for many reasons. Foundational years are important because they pave the way for later. Good parenting means starting early and staying consistent. These building block years are so important to how a kid learns behavior and interacts with others. Truly every year matters and we believe in a no-nonsense parenting style that starts as soon as babies are born. Habits start early.

Having a baby for the first time is 100% being in unfamiliar water. There is no real way to know what is like until you are actually there. We laugh now but my husband looked at me when we took our first born home and said "what are we supposed to do now?" I think I said something like "I'm sure we'll figure it out." The truth is that I love kids--always have, and I was thrilled to now be a mom. It truly felt natural to me and I was amazed that we now had our own little bundle of joy. I couldn't wait to get him home and start the never-ending process of being a mom, a parent. I loved every minute of it (still do) and believe that parenting is probably the most important (and hardest) job anyone will ever do.

What I wasn't ready for was the sleep deprivation and the physical demands on new parents. You have to lift, carry, move, haul, and all types of equipment comes with it all. You have to put things together. You have to fold up strollers and cram them into your car. You have to figure out how carseats work and you have to deal with safety devices and all types of baby contraptions. If you are lucky you may get a stretch of four hours sleep now and then. Sound about right?

I will admit that I think having my career well-established before having kids was a plus for me in the parenthood category. My work taught me a lot about people and helped prepare me for recognizing what traits are most important. I worked with a lot of good people and watched "successful" families raise great kids. I also saw families who weren't as fortunate for a number of reasons. I studied people and how they interacted in meetings. I watched men with giant egos put people down in public, I guess making themselves feel superior. When I saw this I always thought "I'd hate to be married to that." The workforce definitely is a melting pot from which you will interact with others. These interactions can help hone your parenting skills later. I am grateful for all of the workplace experiences--both good and bad--I had before having my children because I think they were learning opportunities and helpful to me in many ways. For example, just about the time I had our son I was working with a bunch of lawyers. That will certainly toughen you up and thicken your skin!

I remember the very first time I had to correct our son. He wasn't quite one yet and he thought it funny to try and roll while I changed his diaper. As any parent knows, some diapers are way worse than others. After telling him "no" a lot and struggling with it, one day I popped his little bare bottom with my hand and he jolted still, looked at me in shock and then those big tears came (now after I got his diaper on him I held him close and comforted him telling him that I didn't want to spank him but he can't do that...followed by kisses and a story to change the subject, he recovered fine) I guess that was his first "spanking" experience but certainly not his last. So I'm just going to tell you right now that I disagree with all the "experts" who claim that spanking is not the way to discipline your child. I am not proclaiming to be a child development PhD here so it is possible that I am wrong, but I doubt it. At least I wasn't wrong about my own kids--they needed spanking some and it worked. By the time our son was 4, he knew for sure what our values were and he really did not require much spanking later. We also used "time outs" although I think that worked better on our daughter than our son.

One time, I remember our daughter, Abby, had done something repeatedly against our rules (I can't recall what she did) and my husband, Jim, told her to go upstairs and wait for him in her bathroom. I think she was maybe 6 or 7. She reluctantly went upstairs and while waiting for Jim to come spank her, proceeded to pad her underwear with mounds of toilet paper and then put on two pairs of pants to shield between her bottom from

Jim's hand. I don't know how he suppressed his laughter, but he managed to "spank" her (he acted like he didn't notice the extra 20 lbs she had on) and that was that. Clearly she got a spanking but it couldn't have possibly hurt. I think girls are more creative earlier in their ability to try and throw parents off course. I also remember one time Bryan telling me that my spankings didn't even hurt. So funny to me now! Later, when our kids outgrew spankings (and I think they do to some extent) we would revoke privileges if we had to make a point.

Another thing we tend to do, in the south especially, is teach manners and respect and we want our kids to say "yes Ma'am and no Sir" to adults. My parents drilled this into me and I said that to every single adult and still do. Properly and respectfully speaking to others and good manners were of HIGH value in our family. Looking people in the eye when you speak to them is also of value. We have passed that on to our kids who were also raised addressing and answering adults in a respectful way. I am mortified by the fact that there are kids who assault adults in school and other places. We have to do better.

My parents also would tell us that if "you don't have anything nice to say, just don't say anything." That is a great piece of advice that I have tried to honor and stay true to. Sometimes it is difficult but it gets to the point of teaching our kids when to pick their battles. I don't believe in never saying what needs saying or staying quiet when you know you shouldn't. I just think there's a time for it and you have to know the difference. There is also the point of respecting differences and knowing that others will disagree which is fine as long as we respect each other's opinions (we don't have to agree) and their right to speak them.

I have a saying that I still use which is "good children get more privileges." I will tell that to any young parent who will give me five minutes to listen. The better your kids become (knowing the rules and values and living by them) the more freedom they will get to have. It's simple. If you trust your kids to do the right things and they demonstrate that they are, then you will allow them more rope. If they choose to hang themselves with it, they will suffer the consequences. And that's really true in life if you think about it. If you are an employer and you have a good employee who always performs, does a good job, etc. isn't that the employee you want to promote? Doesn't that employee get more pay than the one who doesn't perform?

I focus writing about discipline and routine in the foundational years here because I assume most parents do all the other things well. These include things like feeding them, bathing them, loving and holding your babies often (which I did constantly). I must have kissed each baby a million times a day. I can remember one day sitting on my front porch after Bryan woke up from his nap and holding him in my lap. He twisted, wiggled, and wanted down so I let him down and remember thinking, "so the independence begins so young." Hold those babies, kiss them, read to them, play with them, tickle them, laugh with them, toss them up in the air and catch them (while you can) and enjoy every single minute. Blink and they are getting a driver's license.

When your children are young, often they get sick and cannot describe how they feel. I cannot stress enough the importance of a good pediatrician. In our family, we are, by nature, slow to panic, but when you need a good doctor, you need one. Many babies have ear infections, get colds and sometimes just have trouble digesting formula or baby foods. As parents, we want to resolve whatever is hurting them quickly! Back in the day when our kids were babies, we didn't have facebook or any digital sites where we could ask our friends questions. Take advantage of the advice of other parents out there who have been there and ask.

I remember thinking (and still do) that God knows exactly what He is doing. If you think about it, 9 months is about right for a pregnancy. The first month you are excited--and afraid too--but by month 9, you'll do just about anything to get that baby out, right? By the time your child wants to express himself by wiggling and wrestling to get down off your lap, independence is coming and crawling leads to walking at just the right time. When they are 5, aren't you ready for them to go to kindergarten? By the time they are 16, they need that driver's license! You may need it more than they do! And when they hit about 18, aren't you ready for them to "launch" to college? Hopefully never to permanently return to live under your roof. Yes, God has a great sense of timing and the truth is, it goes by so fast. That's why these early years are so very critical.

The early years are also the years when you see the world again--if you look--through your child's eyes and senses. It was so wonderful to see our babies see a dog or a cat for the first time. To see a baby laugh as a dog licks him while he's in his bouncy seat. The pure joy that lights up a child's face when they get to hold and have something they want, like a puppy. I loved those precious, fleeting moments. Children--as they are naturally curious and always discovering can teach us so much. This discovery journey I think makes us better parents and really, better people. Children teach us that the simple things bring us the most joy. Having my own children forced me to recall my childhood and remember some of the things we did as a family. That reflection can bring both positive and negative feelings back but for me, they were mostly positive. It is important to find joy in the moment and cherish positive memories.

I remember well the day I took Abby to pick out a puppy from a labrador breeder we had selected. Abby was almost 5 years old (such a fun age) and the two of us set off to go "pick out" one of the seven or eight yellow lab puppies. There is nothing better than watching your child sit down and have numerous, adorable wiggly, licking puppies climb all over you.

Abby was set on the big yellow, fluffy one and also the one who would not stop biting on her cowboy boot. Abby wore pink pants, brown boots and a white shirt to pick out her puppy. She named it "Jazz" and that dog was her dog from the get go. It would ride with her in her electric "Barbie" car until it was too large to fit.

Here are some things I can recall with both of our kids that we did right in the early years:

- Kept a consistent bedtime schedule and stuck to it; we valued routine and sleep. People don't know this but kids grow when they sleep
- Read to them. Read to your babies and young children every chance you get! Studies have shown that reading to them often is one of the best paths to their success in school and life
- Supported them emotionally and listened to them--be their biggest cheerleaders
- Once we said "no" we stuck to it even if we had doubts--we also agreed early that we were united in our approach: If I said "no" then Jim backed me up and vice versa: Kids will try to get one parent to say "yes" and our kids had a rule early on which was that if one parent said "no" that stood for both and they better not try and go get another answer of there would be trouble
- Required nap time, reading time and quiet time when they were really young
- Taught them safety tips early: human trafficking is real. Teach them that adults don't ask kids for help, directions or assistance. If you don't know what to do, ask anyone who works with kids and find resources on this subject
- Had family nights where kids get to pick food and help cook: be present

- Let them have pets if you can: there is nothing better than puppies and young children and it teaches them responsibility when they are old enough to have them (after 6 or 7 is probably better than 5)
- Made them play outside (we moved to a rural area so they could); went fishing
- Encouraged learning to play music; our son took guitar lessons in elementary school
- Made them do chores and clean their rooms
- Taught them to respect themselves, others and elders
- Spanked them when they needed it
- Let siblings fight it out unless they are really hurting each other
- Explained the why behind the "no"--talk to kids and explain why they cannot do something and what you think and then get them to express what they think
- Didn't overextend and overschedule: my rule was 1 sport at a time (God bless the parents who have sons in competitive baseball and daughters in soccer)
- Dropped EVERYTHING when they needed us: sick, hurt, bullied, whatever--we were there for them and they came first
- Said no to other parents and always checked with parents as to whereabouts of kids
- Rejoiced when they said they were bored: long road trips are especially good bonding time
- Ignored bad behavior sometimes--kids will use bad behavior for attention too
- Taught them manners, kindness and the importance of being kind to others
- Spent lots of family time together--anywhere. It doesn't need to be elaborate or expensive. Kids want time with their parents and you only have until they hit about 16 to do this

- Loved and embraced being a parent. Don't worry about missing out on social things. Actually our "social" life centered more around our kids' friends and sports so we met new people and made new friends

About Happiness:

While writing this book, I was having a conversation with Abby about what makes people happy. We were talking about how we have both known people who depend on others to make them happy. During the conversation, Abby made the simple point that your own happiness comes from you and nobody can make you happy but yourself. Bingo! I mention it here because when we start a family, often times we think a baby or children will make us happy. They do of course, but they are not the panacea for one's happiness in general. And neither is your spouse for that matter. In fact, some studies have shown that women with children often view their husbands as an extension of the children (a large child) due to chores and housework that comes with raising a family (and that often falls on the women). If you are not happy, do not think that having children will make you happy. Happiness must come from within us. I think we find our own happiness by loving ourselves enough to love others. I think true happiness comes when we let go of jealousy, hate and hypocrisy. Happy people are grateful, generous and positive. I would also go as far to say that I think happy people make great parents. Our kids need and deserve happiness.

About sports and raising children:

I have always been an advocate of the "one thing at a time" rule which also includes involvement in sports. Our son played baseball for awhile and once he finally admitted to us that it was not a passion, he stopped (and we got our weekends back). Our daughter ran track and cross country (and did some other various sports early on) but our family schedules were never dictated by sports. I think every family has to do what is right for them and for us, sports were viewed as something fun to dabble in but not required. We didn't push our kids to do sports for several reasons (Again, every family must do what is right for them and their child. If one of our children had expressed undying passion for a sport and demonstrated a gift at it, we would have supported that).

First, we are older parents and we don't like baking in the sun for hours on a Saturday watching multiple games of baseball or worse--watching a track and field day. While we certainly supported our kids, we--the parents--didn't feel the need to re-live our childhood vicariously through our kids. And we certainly noted those parents who did! You know the ones who yell at the coaches at games--it always amazed me to witness it. When our son stopped playing baseball, we got our weekends back (and many nights during the week) and started enjoying family time on the Tennessee River.

Another reason we didn't push our kids is because they are under enough pressure already these days. It was hard enough being a kid back in the 70's. I cannot imagine doing it now! I know sports help build confidence and self esteem in kids, but I think sometimes too much of that can be a bad thing. I also think that it depends on the kid. As parents, we have to know our children--what inspires them, what helps them, what limits them, etc. While one kid may thrive in competitive baseball, a sibling may not. Every child is different--even within a family. Our kids have much in common but they are also very different. Knowing what motivates your kids is half the battle. Listening to them, understanding them and supporting them is the other half.

As teen sports has become a huge business where a lot of money is being made, I would challenge parents to ask, "is it worth it?" If your son or daughter doesn't have a passion to be the best in a particular sport, is it really going to net you any real return on that investment (of both time and money)? And in today's new world, competition is rather fierce with trainers and technology, kids are being pushed to be better, faster, stronger. Personally, I think it's too much but that's just my opinion and experience--I'm certain many parents would disagree and demonstrate the other side of this but that's okay too. It's worth the dialogue.

I remember when Bryan was a junior in high school on the varsity trap team and he made a comment that he wasn't going to shoot on the team his senior year. I remember saying "Oh yes you certainly will. You are going to finish what you started and one more year will not hurt you." This was one of the only times I can remember standing my ground involving a team sport. My message to him was you don't quit something at the end and let the team down. He finished strong and helped lead his trap team at Houston High. It was a fun group of friends and he was also good at shooting and the team needed every shooter they had.

About academics:

I could write an entire book on this subject and probably so could most parents. Looking back, sometimes I wonder how we got through all the homework and "projects" and testing, etc. that kids go through in school. Taking into consideration the many types of academic experiences out there (private, public, home school, boarding school) I think our kids are missing out on a lot in school. Curriculum needs to be constantly challenged and we need to get back to the basics of reading, writing, math and science. We need less reliance on scholastic testing as the single most important measuring stick of a student's potential and ability. A test score--while used by schools as either an entry or barrier to it--cannot, in my opinion, measure the academic potential of a student.

Finally, we need to take political and social agendas out of schools. Schools who coddle kids and only "lean" left or right are missing the point. Our students need to consider different viewpoints so they can learn to think for themselves. Too many schools (colleges) are breeding grounds for political action, propaganda, and recently, even the limitation of free speech. Hogwash, to all of that I tell you! Students on college campuses should not feel threatened, bullied or unsafe to voice a differing opinion than that of which the institution may hold. We have seen many recent examples of violence across college campuses of late. This must stop or else we will see an increase in online degrees and a decline in college admissions.

When my kids were in elementary school, I would get so frustrated as a parent that they would come home with so much homework. Mounds of it! And working parents (especially single parents) don't have time to come home, fix dinner and figure out how to do a worksheet they did 30 years ago. I got so mad one day that I actually wrote and submitted an op-ed piece that ran in our local paper. It got a lot of traction and many like-minded parents reached out to me and said they agreed. There were some too, who didn't agree with me and that's fine. I think they are referred to as "helicopter parents," which we are not.

In our first book, "Women in High Gear," we write about the STEM (science, technology, engineering and math) being a demonstrated and proven path for girls in particular to grow up and get to the C-suite (CEO, COO, CFO, CIO, CMO). Historically, STEM courses have been male-dominated. We believe that girls should aspire to disciplined academics such as science and math. These are tougher subjects for many (me included) but we should encourage our children--no matter the gender--to pursue these subjects, especially if they have the acumen for them. I think schools should focus on teaching as many of our kids the basics well. And they should do it while the kids are actually in school. And put American history--as it actually happened--back into our school systems. Enough of the watering down of American history due to hurt feelings and political correctness--like a cancer to our country.

To teachers, educators and school administrators: As parents, we would like for you to teach our children these foundational subjects while you have them under your roof. You have them most of their waking hours and they need to actually be learning while they are at school. It's not our job to do yours. If a parent has a child in a private school that costs a lot of money, they don't expect to have to re-teach or teach a subject. I remember when our son was briefly in a private middle school. We put him there because we thought he'd do better there. Unfortunately, the $18k we spent for the 6th grade might have as well been flushed down the toilet (with the exception of some lifelong friends that he made while there). He was struggling in a few subjects. After some parent-teacher meetings, the teachers suggested we hire a private tutor. I thought to myself "maybe he wouldn't have to have one if they would do their jobs." We voted with our feet and left that school and went back to public school for high school. It ended up being a very good decision for many reasons.

And I remember one important thing about that year at that school. Other mothers were telling me that maybe Bryan needed to be tested or needed to be on medication, etc. He just was not a good student and we were worried (oh the pressure!). So many of his friends were being prescribed adderall and we just wanted to steer away from that. I kept saying "we all made it through school without medications so why should cave to the pressure and do that?" I remember calling our pediatrician, who set up an appointment, evaluated Bryan and concluded that Bryan was a normal 6th grade BOY which meant he didn't want to be cooped up in a classroom with books all day. Suddenly something that seemed so mysterious and serious was comical and practical. OF COURSE!

Parents of boys: if they don't like school, that's probably normal. It doesn't mean letting them off the hook, but it explains why they tell you they don't have homework when they actually do. It explains why the want to go outside and play. Boys need action. They need to be doing something with their little bodies and sitting behind a desk is counter-productive for them in 6th grade! In that very same school that we left, some teacher--who probably didn't have kids--made them read a really boring book for summer reading. Even I thought it was boring and I thought, "why make them read that boring stuff?" If the point is to encourage reading, let them read what inspires them, right? After the book report was submitted, Bryan asked my husband if we could put the book in the skeet thrower, launch it in the air and "shoot it to pieces" which, of course, we did. Somehow word got back to the school about the skeet thrower and shooting up the book. I don't think they thought that was funny but we sure did.

Parents, don't do your child's homework either. Help them if they need it but don't be sucked into helping them to the point of doing it. Not only are they not learning it but they aren't learning how to be responsible for their "to do" list. When our youngest hit middle school, I stopped helping her with her homework. We must have told our kids many times that we had already been through 6th grade and we weren't going back. Kids need to learn how to balance and be responsible. Often, when one of ours left something it home they needed, I was not in a position to take it. Tough love but important if your child is going to learn to be accountable.

At some point, we stopped packing our kids' lunches and they would either do it themselves or their laziness or forgetfulness would result in them eating the school food. My point is that kids have to be responsible for their school work and get it done, turned in, etc. Middle school is a good time for them to start learning how to be responsible for those daily tasks. Their brains are still developing (more on that later) and if nothing else repetition is important and getting into good habits should be formed early. And at about middle school we stopped taking forgotten items to the school. If our kid forgot their homework, well, too bad. They probably wouldn't again. If they don't have some skin in the game, they won't learn.

And about these "projects"....what are we teaching them? If a teacher assigns a project that a child likely cannot do on their own, guess who gets to? Right! The parents! I hated--with a passion--school projects. Thankfully, the school my daughter is finishing high school in, assigns them as a team so the kids work together. As working parents, we don't have time to do our kids work and we shouldn't want to. Schools who assign mountains of homework are missing the boat. Homework should only be for extra help with a subject or as a reminder. Kids should not have too much of it either. If they play a sport AND have homework, they don't get much sleep and forget having dinner as a family. What we really need more of is family time!

Do you know what a former DEA agent who locked up drug dealers and bad guys for years said about our kids? They don't have the magic number 7: 7 nights around a dinner table talking with their parents. His name is Robert Stutman (The Stutman Group) and you can Google him and watch his video. He is an expert on our opioid drug problem in teens (more about that later) and he attributes kids turning to drugs to escape. We have too much pressure on our kids today. As parents, we need to communicate with our kids--especially in high school when they can drive. Homework piled on for the sake of educators patting themselves on the back for high test scores is hurting our kids.

I'd rather my kids love a subject and genuinely be interested in it than have great grades across the board so they can get into an exclusive college. The **passion for learning and wanting to** is where we need to focus.

About daycare and childcare:

One of the struggles many families have is how to provide childcare for young children, especially if both parents have to work (and today, most do). We had our oldest in a church daycare center five days a week (I was working full-time even though I owned my own business) until I found a woman to come to my home and help me. Yes, it is expensive but after the second one came, it about evened out. It was more affordable to have a "nanny" than to truck two toddlers to daycare. I remember one day I had just dressed Bryan for the day, dressed myself (in a suit back then because I worked with lawyers) and loaded up his diaper bag for the day to tote him to daycare when he spit up a full 8 oz. of formula right down my shirt. It was at that moment that I decided I was done with daycare and my search for the nanny began. The nice thing about the nanny situation was that she agreed to get to my house each day by 7:30 a.m. so I could finish getting ready and my child could stay in his pj's and his own environment and not have a bottle shoved down him so I could get him to daycare on time. Later, at some point we did "mother's day out" a few days a week to expose him to other kids (and give the nanny a break). At first he didn't like it but after the first two weeks, he loved it.

Every family must do what is right for them. Fortunately, daycares and childcare options are much better today than they were 20 years ago but they are also more expensive. It was recently reported that the average family spends 30% of its after tax money annually on daycare. That is huge! As some suspect, maybe this is why more women (women make up 47% of the American workforce) opt out and stay home to take care of kids.

For us, having someone come to the house was our solution. Expensive yes, but I had to work and I wanted to work. My income exceeded what we spent on childcare and not working would have hurt our family more financially.

About potty training:
I think one benefit of being an "older" parent (I was 32 when I had my first) was we just didn't get all worked up about this. Boys will potty train a bit later than girls, but each kid is different. What we ended up doing was using PULL-UPS! They are the best invention ever. Just as our kids were able to use the potty, we put them in pull-ups and just let them figure it out. We definitely put them on them at night and if they wet them, so what. We never worried about it, made an issue of it and if they wet the bed, we just stripped it and washed the sheets. I did put a plastic liner under each kids' mattress pad but the truth is--they will wet the bed. If you make a big deal out of it, it will become one. Just put them in pull-ups and forget it! They'll grow out of it.

A funny side story here we still laugh about. When Abby was a baby and could sit in the tub in one of those safety suction chairs, we would often bathe the kids at the same time (efficiency). Bryan was 4 and Abby was say 8-10 months. Neither one wanted to get out of the tub (most kids love the water) and we would have all kinds of toys and stuff in the tub. The bath time was something I looked forward to but knew it would be followed by reading time so eventually, we knew they had to get out of the tub. One night my prankster husband grabbed a handful of raisins and while our son was not looking, tossed them in the tub and said, "Look, poop!" Bryan shot out of the tub like a rocket. We love that story and laugh about it all the time. When Bryan was "potty training" he informed me that there were two kinds of poop: train poop and raisin poop. Pretty funny. Hey, when you have babies, there is a LOT of poop talk! It's just part of it.

Your Children are NOT your Life:

Parents beware of centering all of your attention on your children. A healthy marriage makes for good parenting. Be sure to make time for you and your spouse. My Dad, the retired Presbyterian preacher (and current Grandfather "Papa" to our kids) used to say this sentence all the time: "The best thing a father can do for his children is love their mother." Don't you just love that? I know it goes both ways, but that generation grew up very differently from ours. But this is true. Kids see and learn by watching parents. They know when things aren't right and when a parent is stressed.

Honesty:

We talk to our kids a lot about problems if we have them and have been very transparent with them as they have aged. My husband and I were unfortunately both in bad first marriages. Both of us divorced our ex-spouses and thankfully neither one of us had kids by the first marriages. Later, when our kids were old enough we told them that we had both been married to other people (we refer to that as "our previous lives with our outlaws"). Their first response: "do we have any half-brothers or sisters that we don't know about?" The second came from my daughter "Are there any other big secrets you aren't telling us about in your past?" We laughed hard at that one. The truth is, no marriage is perfect and no one person is either. We all make mistakes and learning from them and moving forward is the thing that matters most. And being honest with our kids is important to us.

When our kids ask us questions about other things like money or things happening in other families, we try hard to be honest and help them understand. Sometimes their questions mean something is bothering them and they want more discussion. Or maybe they ask because they think it applies to them. Our son is very sensitive and aware of monetary issues (always has been) and--although they didn't grow up poor--they know how hard we have worked and they appreciate what they have. Not all kids do. You cannot teach your kids what it's like to be poor unless you are poor. Both of us grew up in families that made it work by the hardest sometimes. I won't go as far as to say we lived in poverty, but we had to save and work to make it. And our parents certainly didn't have extra money for ski trips or big vacations. Jim remembers living in a house that didn't have central air and heat (that's how old he is--lol, just kidding). That's a hard thing to translate to our own children, but we have done our best. I think every parent wants to give their kids a life better than what they had. I'm not sure that's a good thing. Lots of good lessons in being "not rich" and having to sacrifice and work for things. Our society puts so much value on success, money and power and material possessions--the pressure to be successful is real. I know we have worked hard to make sure our kids don't put too much stock in this. I have a sign over my back door that reads: "The best things in life aren't things."

Good parenting means translating important values early so that when they hit 20, they have had years of understanding them. As an example, one time about nine years ago we were all at dinner with friends (parents and all kids). It was a fairly upscale restaurant and the menu prices were high. One of the other kids wanted to order the "bone-in-ribeye steak" which was priced at $58.00 (and that didn't include any side items). He didn't get to and I was so relieved his parents said "no." How many 13-year olds need that? Even today when we go out to eat, our kids will ask if it's "okay" for them to order something a bit more pricey. Or, often they'll agree to split something. The fact that they ask and are aware of the cost is fantastic!

One of the absolute best things you can teach your kids is for them to have to ask often, "Is there anything I can do to help?" We taught our kids and others who came to our river house as guests to ask this. Remember, it becomes habit. The payoff is that as they age, they actually do become helpers and it teaches them that if they are a guest in your house or another's, they pull their weight. Kids need to learn the basics of chores and so by teaching them to ask, "Is there anything I can do to help?" you are doing them a great service. They'll be more likely to be a team player later in the workforce too.

Blended Families:
We don't have one so we cannot know what it is like but we have friends who do. Some of our kids friends have blended families. All I can say here is that I have a lot of respect for people who make things work when dealing with blended family "issues." It is stressful enough raising kids with your own flesh and blood family. I cannot imagine trying to raise kids when you have ex-spouses and in-law influences to deal with. I have watched some of my dear friends manage this with class and grace. The main thing my friends of blended families say is that they do everything in the best interests of the kids. Admirable and stressful at the same time.

About Lying:
In our family, we taught our kids that if they lied to us, that would be a bigger deal than whatever it was they did. I have zero tolerance for liars. Liars cannot be trusted and therefore will have troubled relationships along their life journey. We put the hammer down early on our kids about lying. It truly is one of the most destructive of habits. Teach your kids early on the importance of telling the truth--no matter what. Once they know they are safe for telling you the truth, they will know that you value truth over any negative

consequences of their actions. In other words, we told our kids that no matter what happened or what they did, we wanted the truth. They also learned the hard way what would happen if they got caught in a lie. I can only remember one time when I caught one of them in a lie over something very trivial. Although the action was trivial, the lie was not. The lie became the big focus and I made sure to make it a big deal with punishment that included revoked privileges and a written "essay" on why one should not lie. It worked and I still have the written essay in an 8 year old's handwriting.

WIC and HIP phase:
My husband nicknamed both of our kids, Bryan became "WIC" and Abby was "HIP": Bryan was Wic for "Walks in Circles" and Abby was Hip for "Hands in Pockets"--Wic meant walking around aimlessly not accomplishing anything and Hip meant not helping (you can't work if your hands are in your pockets). They outgrew this phase but we still tease them about it. If you have teens you know they go through that phase of walking around, opening the refrigerator and staring aimlessly into it as if by magic--if you stand there long enough--a hand holding a hot meal with appear. Or they'll open the food pantry and stand there looking as if their brain is trying to process what is there. Or they forget to take their stuff up the stairs as you swear you will break your neck tripping over it for the tenth time. It does actually, finally, all come together as that frontal lobe develops.

Teach them to grow something and love Mother Earth:
You don't have to be a farmer to teach your kids to love and respect nature and all of her beauty. Simple gardening in your backyard in summer months, planting flowers and herbs in the spring...all of these small things can impress upon kids the importance of harvesting and living off the land. We always plant tomatoes and peppers in the summer and recently, turnip

greens in the fall. We have friends who also have gardens and there is nothing better than tasting that freshly picked produce. When we moved out of the city and to a more rural area, our yard has a small lake/pond on it and we taught our kids (and their friends) to fish. As our kids grew, it wasn't uncommon for them to haul a bunch of bass up the hill to clean and cook! Some of my favorite memories are of our son and his friends walking down the hill--fishing poles in hand--to go see what they could catch.

Hunting can also be beneficial in teaching kids how to manage land as farms have different programs to ensure proper game management. Hunting has been a big part of our family over the years and taught our kids respect for animals and the land and how to take good care of both. Understanding that our food sources don't just come from the grocery store is a way to give your kids something they can fall back on if they had to or wanted to. And I have great, massive respect for farmers and ranchers. I love the bumper stickers that say "No Farms, No Food." Thanks to my friend Pam for reminding me to include this in the book!

Never Give up and Laugh:
One of the most important things about parenting is that you never give up. It is a job you have forever. Parents who give up on their kids maybe shouldn't have had them in the first place. As parents we must never give up on our kids. Giving up is not an option. If you need help, get help but don't ever quit parenting. If you fall down seven times, you get up eight. Parenting is a marathon, not a sprint. There are days when you will think you can't make it, but keep going forward. Keep trying and before you know it, you'll be another mile or so down the road and onto a new view. The teen years can be very trying for parents. Keep going, be consistent and stick to your values. The awkward days, hormonal induced drama days and arguments will pass. Remember that you--the parent--are in charge no

matter how creative or persuasive the teens can be. Draw upon that courage you have down deep that says "I am the boss of you and I will outwork you. I may not be as fast, but I'm wise." Remember, you are the parent, not the pal. And if you give an inch, they'll take a mile. And they are persuasive, creative and can sense any fear, second-guessing or doubts you are having. Don't give in. Trust your gut and wisdom and use your own creativity when you can.

And embrace what is funny. Kids are funny, especially when they are little. In their quest and zeal for learning, they can say and do things that are hilarious.

This reminds me of a story. When Abby was in middle school and Bryan was maybe a freshman or sophomore in high school, somebody was definitely leaving Capri Sun straw wrappers everywhere and empty boxes in the refrigerator. We were picking up those damn, clear wrappers to the point of hearing "we're not buying drinks anymore" out of my own mouth everyday. We blamed Bryan. One day (after tired of being blamed of course) Bryan set up a hidden camera in the kitchen area and caught Abby red-handed coming in from school, getting the last Capri Sun out, leaving the empty box, and throwing the wrapper up in the air as she jammed the straw into the packet, going about her merry way. BUSTED. Not only did Bryan film it, he made a "crime video" of it adding music and repeating the part where she throws the wrapper up in slow motion--it is hilarious! And to make the whole thing even funnier, it was "nerd" day at Abby's school that day, so in the video she is featured in full nerd-regalia committing the "family crime." Priceless. When I want a good laugh, I watch that video. And, of course, Bryan was fully vindicated and reminds us often.

Laugh at the ridiculous. I found that sometimes my teens would be shocked when I would laugh at some of the things they said. Whether it was for attention or to make me mad, when I laughed, it seemed to diffuse their little fire. It wasn't the reaction they expected and that element of surprise can be a great parenting tactic. Another tactic is to ignore them when you need to and pretend you have something more important to do and/or attend to when they pull something dumb. I'm sure this is probably one of the things I learned having young staff at work. When you have hired and trained a bunch (over my 30 year career) of young people, it gives you great parenting experience. The phrase "I'm going to pretend I didn't just hear that," was always a good one because it diffused the issue and put the ownership on the one who said something stupid--which is constant when raising kids and training young staff. There is nothing wrong with them, they just don't know what they don't know.

Write things down! I wrote things down the kids said when they were little (not as much now) and it is hysterical to go back and read. I love and admire the parents who have the discipline to keep written journals. One year our Christmas card was a photo of our kids and on the back was a list of the funniest things they had said that year (something different, right?). The only one I remember is this: We had a yellow lab named Harley (female) who had a slipped disc in her back. We had taken her to the vet and that was the report. She would heal fine but try those words on a 6-year old. Our son went around telling everyone (often when we weren't around to correct it) that "Harley had a slipped dick." Remember, Harley was female. People were calling me to report it and laugh with me. This was one of the funniest things Bryan said innocently and without purpose of being funny.

Laughter is truly good medicine and an important part of raising good kids. Write funny things they say down in a book or you'll forget them. As their little brains are churning, growing and they are capable of figuring things out faster, our brains are deteriorating. Trust me, you forget.

About the mood swings and middle school:

Sometimes I hear parents say things like "where did my sweet child go?" Or "they were smarter when they were 4." Or "I don't know why my daughter is so annoyed with me all the time." Relax parents (I know, easier said than done) but this too shall pass. I'm no psychologist, but after reading "The Teenage Brain" I think they just cannot help it. I'm sure we were like this as well. The truth is that middle school and pre-puberty years are not always a picnic. We didn't have too much of it (or maybe I just blocked it out or forgot it) but kids go through a natural period of figuring out who they are and what they need. They slam doors, talk back, disappear for hours into their rooms (which are disaster zones and science projects) and walk around in circles. It's normal. As long as they don't cross the line and violate boundaries and established house rules (ground rules as my parents always said) they'll grow out of it. Somehow around about the age range of 17 and 20 they start to come back to you. They seem to become nicer and more helpful too. It's easy to feel like you are failing at parenting when your kids go through these phases. What is important is to be consistent, try and ignore the small stuff (pick your battles) and forget some of it. Chalk it up to hormones and let them stay secluded in their cave if they want. They'll eventually come out in search of food. And when they do, resist the urge to talk. Sometimes as parents, we just need to let them be and they'll talk when they are ready. Just listen.

About the strong-willed child:

There is no doubt in my mind that the strong-willed ones can be the most challenging to parent. In our case, both of ours are strong-willed which I believe to be more of a positive than a negative ultimately (or maybe I should say eventually). And remember, apples don't fall far from the trees so as parents, we must look within ourselves and realize that our kids come by it naturally. We have joked a lot in our family when our kids would do something "strong-willed" we would look at each other and say "he's your child," or "she's just like you." If you have a strong-willed child, you probably know it very early. They push your buttons, push boundaries, test you, and often make you think you are a bad parent. You're not. They are actually making you a better one.

The best advice I can give parents with these kinds of kids is to stay consistent, verbalize your values and boundaries often, and pick your battles. They will manipulate you, use reverse psychology and will even get their friends to help if they think they can have their way. When they are little, it can be the simple things like trying your patience at naptime or throwing something breakable against a wall to get your attention. When they get older, they can be much more clever and creative. One day recently I was working on my laptop when I got a Twitter notification from one of our daughter's friends. It was early in the school day and Abby wanted to get "checked out" at school because of some program and all the kids were getting their parents to check them out. Initially firm in my resolve of NOT allowing for this, I responded to Abby's text that I would not be checking her out "like everyone else's parents were doing." Then I got a tweet from one of her friends. Then another one. "Please Ms.Amy let her out!!! She's in JAIL!!" said the tweet. Another friend tweeted, "Release Abby now #Torture" --pretty funny. Sometimes as parents you have to meet them where they are. I thought about it and tweeted this back at them: "You are staying in school for your fave. #ALGEBRA."

While that strong personality can make you crazy when they are younger, as they age, I believe being strong-willed is a blessing which helps them navigate through life. Butting heads will happen often--especially around high school age, but remember you are the parent, not the pal. We didn't tolerate much backtalk or disrespect for our rules. If our kids did that, we usually responded with a swift correction or taking the car keys away for a weekend. As parents of strong-willed kids, we must harness their passion and help steer them to use that willful power for positivity.

The people who don't have kids:
Not everyone becomes a parent. Along our parenting journey we met people who admitted they never had kids for various reasons: some could not, some married too late in life, some never married and some just don't like kids. When I was in my twenties, I couldn't imagine anyone not wanting to become a parent. Now that I am in my fifties, I totally get it. While I love being a parent, I also respect those who are not--even those who don't want to be.

CHAPTER 3
Smartphones: Good, Bad, Ugly

> *"To teach your kids online safety, you have to let them go online. That's a scary prospect for parents but you need to supervise their first experiences with the Internet and help to know which kinds of behavior raises red flags. It's like if you had a pool in your yard and told the kids they couldn't go near it: they'd likely sneak in when you weren't looking and that's incredibly dangerous. As a parent, it's my responsibility to help my kids learn to safely navigate the waters (literally and figuratively)."*
> --KERRY O'SHEA GORGONE (DIGITAL NINJA, SOCIAL MEDIA BLOGGER, WRITER, GREAT PARENT AND FRIEND IN REAL LIFE AND ONLINE)

In our second book, "Students in High Gear" we wrote a lot about this topic--mainly to help high school and college students so that they are ***employable*** after college. The truth is that our kids' "digital footprint" or "digital tattoo" starts as soon as they get a smartphone. Poof! Just like that, our kids have the power of the internet in their pockets--although we'd argue the phones never make it there as they are in hand constantly. Go to any public place where there are teens and look around at what they are doing. They are selfie-snapchatting and instagramming their lives away and churning through your data plan. The amount of data, distractions, communications that is thrown at them must be overwhelming to them. We cannot imagine having to go through the teen years with a smartphone and the internet. And we hear all the time this phrase from adults our age, "It's a good thing we didn't grow up with iPhones when we were in school." Yes, times have changed.

We didn't have cell phones or the internet when we were kids. Think about that. We are parenting kids who have more technology in their hand than the White House did when we were in college. There is just no way to keep our children offline so we must equip them with the knowledge they need to navigate this crazy digital, information-everywhere world. It's truly hard to think about sometimes. I am an advocate for using social media for good and for business. I use the internet daily and am constantly overwhelmed by the things I read and see. Bottom line? Our kids are too.

I have a power point I give when I talk to middle schools called "The 10 Commandments of Posting Online." When I started speaking to schools six or seven years ago, I realized that high school was too late. I needed to talk to kids in middle schools--when many are getting phones. Parents need to understand what these social media tools are and how they are being used.

You cannot keep up with every single app or social channel out there. You must teach your kids that no matter what they use (because it will forever be changing), what matters is what they post. You can't guard all the bridges and we are sticking our heads in the sand if we think we can. I talk to parents often who say things like "I have a tracker on my daughter's phone" or "I get into their phones to see what they are saying…" REALLY? Is this how you parent? Because kids are smart and savvy about this. And if you go behind their backs, is that really the way you want to parent? Do you think that builds trust? They will only let you see what you think you need to see. So what do we do as parents? Just like anything else, you trust them, verify by asking them, and teach them to do the right things online.

And how many times has your teen son or daughter walked in and fixed the remote or something on your phone or computer that you had been struggling with for hours? Kids today are tech-savvy and their brains actually enable them to figure things out faster than adults. It's proven neuroscience so don't feel slighted when this happens. It is really freeing to know that this is natural. We often get so frustrated by technology but to teens it is intuitive. So we can give them our wisdom and they can help us with the technology. But don't think you can outsmart them with their technology.

What we as parents can give them is our wisdom and experience and we need to start when they are young. I started lecturing my kids as I prepared for these talks at various schools and I used my kids as guinea pigs to see how they liked what I said. The best tip I got from my oldest was that if I was going to "give a boring lecture on telling us what to do and not do (picture eye-rolling here) that I should at least bring good candy." The good candy was a hit--good tip from my son!

Here is my advice to parents on the topic of smartphones and kids:

- Start early--as soon as they get the phone
- Set rules and guidelines: I know some parents who take their kids phones away at a certain hour at night; we didn't but probably should have
- Tell your kids that you trust them until they give you a reason not to (remember, good kids get more freedom)
- Tell your kids that anything they post can be found--anything

- Go through examples of what is appropriate to post and what is not: be specific
- Coaches, recruiters, employers are all looking at our kids' "digital footprint"
- Communicate often about this with your kids. If you see something, say something and make sure they understand the "why" behind the "don't do that"
- Google social media policy and guidelines and show what you find to your kids
- Have a police officer come talk to the kids as a group about the real life dangers online and things they have to deal with daily (pedofilia and human trafficking are real)
- Make sure you kids understand the security settings and use them
- Ask your PTA or school if they host any talks or provide resources or counseling
- Talk with other parents about creative ideas and what they see and do
- Encourage your kids to put their phones down as much as possible
- Mandate dinner at the table with no phones so discussion can happen

Most of this is common sense but the problem with that is that common sense isn't so common. I tell parents to remember this one thing: If you wouldn't want to see it on the front page of a newspaper, don't post it (because that's where it could end up). I expand that to YouTube where something could get millions of views in a short time. **The viral nature of the internet is the new reality we face as we raise our kids.** Think about that for a second. It's a real good reason for birth control. I'm honestly glad our kids are almost grown and it is still frightening to us. A reality is that once they are around 20, they are still not fully developed (brain's frontal lobe) and cannot help being impulsive and/or indecisive. Combine this with every distraction they have on their phones and no wonder kids are getting into so much trouble (for the world to see--literally). Additionally, our kids are at much higher risk for car accidents due to the texting and phone interactions while they are driving. I believe it is a real problem.

The Digital Footprint of our Kids: Parents who Post

I tell parents to also be mindful of what they themselves are posting as well--especially if it's about their children. This is an important part of why I wanted to write this book. We tend to--as parents--focus on teaching our kids what to do and not do but we need to remember the rules as well. When our kids are young, their "digital footprint" is already being created by the parents. You see this of sonogram photos of babies in the womb on Facebook. Then, when they are born, we have all these wonderful digital photos of them. It is great if it is used for good, but dangerous if not. Parents need to be mindful as their kids age of what they are posting about them online. A kid's digital footprint has a long life and we need to be sure we are respecting their privacy and not harming them or risking anything in their futures.

I'll use myself as an example. I try to use a G, PG and R rating system for posting. If my kids were doing something that I want to share, I usually made sure it is G rated. Not harmful, not threatening, not anything that can be misunderstood, misconstrued or used against them. For example, I have steered away from posting hunting photos online as so many people don't like hunting animals. I'm not saying don't be who you want to be online. I'm just saying that as parents, our job is to shield our kids' digital footprint from those who could prevent them from succeeding. I have limited what I have posted as my kids have aged into adults. We need to respect their privacy and also think about what we post. If your son or daughter wants to go into the military, will your posts help them or could they be potentially damaging?

Also, try not to embarrass your kids. I know many of us love to share funny things about our kids but--to them--they aren't funny (especially as they age) or maybe they should stay private. If kids do not feel "safe" at home--the only place that is truly private anymore--then that is a bad thing. Kids need to know that their parents aren't sharing everything about them and that everything they text you won't show up on Facebook. From time to time, I have shared some funny text exchanges but they were harmless to all parties involved. I don't do it often (and as parents of teens you know you could) because I respect their private conversation with me. If your kid wanted all your friends to know something, she could group text them. And to the kids I would remind them the same courtesy would apply. Don't film or photograph your parents and post it without approval as well (although I'm sure I've been the star of many a snapchat post without ever knowing it).

Here are some points for parents (and kids) to consider:

- Respect family privacy
- Ask permission if you want to post a photo first
- Always assume everything is public
- Consider the fact that you are creating your child's "digital footprint" when you post
- Avoid using social media to shame or discipline your child
- Limit posts: not everyone wants to see 45 photos of your child

It's Not Going Away:

As much as sometimes I wish it would all just go away, it's just going to get worse. As tools like snapchat and instagram grow, our kids are in this giant cyclone of instant everything and I don't think that it is good. Kids want information instantly. There is so much information generated about what people are doing that I think it stresses our kids out. I honestly think that some of this is creating anxiety problems in our kids. As parents we need to remind our kids that there is no "perfect" world and that it's okay not to have a "perfect" photo all of the time. This constant documenting of their life has me wondering what kind of adults they will really be. This technology is a real, developing issue, I think.

So as parents, we must accept the reality that kids are going to communicate in mass and often--unless they don't have a smartphone. The other day I heard about a kid who had been involved in a minor wreck and the entire school knew about it before the parents did. Sadly, I recall a fatal crash where a teen was killed and the parents were not the first to know. Stress the importance of your kids communicating often with you. We have always insisted that our kids let us know where they are and when they leave someplace. This becomes habit forming and is just good practice for safety and parenting.

Recently we heard our son say to one of his friends, "let me know which route you are taking so if anything happens we know where to look." He said this to one of his friends who had dropped his phone in the river and was making the two hour drive back home without his phone. I thought my son's statement was brilliant and probably came from years of telling us where he was and when he was leaving someplace. Good habits are formed early.

If kids have phones, they have no reason not to communicate with you. I tell my kids if they don't answer my text messages or phone calls, that I'll swap their phones for a fly phone for emergencies. This doesn't mean you call and text them 24/7 either. Their phones are your leverage. We've taken them away a time or two and trust me, it's a gigantic inconvenience for them but mainly for us!

A real test: A real test is when your college kid calls you first when there is an emergency. I won't go into the specifics of what happened, but I will tell you that we had a recent experience with one of our children who wisely called us for backup at 3:30 in the morning. An ambulance was involved and perhaps a young life was spared. When your kids trust you and feel safe to communicate with you--no matter how dire the situation is-- you have passed a test. As parents, we must do what we can when they are under our rooftops so that when they are not, they will draw on what they learned and even if it is due to fear of not telling you--whatever it takes-- they will make that call. It is also a good reminder to parents with teens and college kids to keep your ringer on your phones ON at night. Their safety is our number one priority and until their frontal lobe in their brains is fully developed (about age 25), we do whatever it takes to keep them safe. Keep your cell phone charged, next to your bed and on.

CHAPTER 4

The Opioid Epidemic, Teen Drinking and Tougher Issues

> *"Hardships often prepare ordinary people for an extraordinary destiny"*
> -- C.S. Lewis

Much has been written about the war on drugs and the opioid epidemic in our country. One of the best resources and experts on this topic is a man named Robert Stutman of The Stutman Group. He is a former DEA (Drug Enforcement Agency of the U. S.) agent and now spends his time speaking around the country to schools, parents and kids about this epidemic. You can find his website at www.TheStutmanGroup.com and read all about him.

Two really good books out there for parents include "How to Raise a Drug-Free Kid," by Joseph A. Califano, Jr. AND "The Teenage Brain," by Dr. Frances E. Jensen (M.D.) with Amy Ellis Nutt. These books shed some great light (and solutions) on this national problem.

Another issue that compounds this epidemic is the consumption of alcohol by teens in our society. According to Stutman, most teens have tasted alcohol by the 4th grade. I don't know about you but that was mind-blowing to hear. As parents we must find helpful resources and equip ourselves with as much information possible to be sure we are raising good kids in a drug and alcohol-pervasive society.

The bottom line is that It's simply all around us and our children are being confronted with it daily. Understanding what is really happening and talking to our kids about it is the start and could mean the difference between life and death.

Former DEA agent now consultant Robert Stutman says that if parents can keep their kids off of drugs until they reach 21 years of age, they have a great chance of never touching drugs. I had the pleasure of hearing him speak and cannot believe some of the statistics and information he shared. It's truly depressing and arguably one of the biggest problems we have with our teens--as a country. 80% of heroin addicts started their addiction by using opioids prescribed to them or someone they knew. We must stop the access to drugs and that starts by admitting to ourselves as parents that drugs are a real deal in the world of teens today. They were real to me in the 70's but not as culturally popular as they seem to be today. I am no expert but I can tell you what we have done and share with you some of our experiences which may help.

Stutman says that drug use starts early and often by teens getting painkillers out of their parents' medicine cabinets. He says that physicians are partly to blame for the epidemic due to them over-prescribing highly addictive pain pills across the board. Kids on sports teams--especially football--are prone to having access to more pain pills and can become easily addicted. Generally, private schools have a higher drug use than public schools, according to Stutman. If you want to know more, all you have to do is talk to a coroner about how many teens end up on a stainless steel slab from "accidental overdose" and/or alcohol poisoning. One of the things the kids do is smash or grind up pills that are meant to be time-released into the bloodstream and ingesting the powder form to have the most impact. Often, these high potency drugs are chased with alcohol (shots) which can be fatal. In doing research for this book, it seemed like almost every parent I talked to knew of someone's teen who had died of accidental overdose. How many kids do we have to bury before we--as a society--wake up and realize we have to educate parents and especially our kids? Further, drug addiction needs to be treated as the disease it is--just like cancer or heart disease. We must focus our efforts on mental health and helping these kids get well. Addiction is an illness, not a behavior. If someone is addicted to drugs, they need medical help from professionals.

Every parent owes it to himself/herself to get educated on what is really happening. There are numerous studies online and more on the way. The number of kids seeking addiction treatment is growing and the ages are getting younger and younger. After I heard Stutman speak, I came home and made dinner, summoned my kids and we sat at the table and I asked them to weigh in on what he had said. My kids confirmed that what Stutman said was true in their circles. It scared me so bad I had to talk to some teachers and school leaders about it to see what else we could be doing. I had to write this book! I had to attend a conference on patient safety and opioid abuse. Some of our schools here are implementing some resources for families who are dealing with teens on drugs--way too many. Another school in our town has started a "speaker series" to help raise awareness for parents and their kids who struggle with alcohol and drug abuse--which often go hand in hand.

As I write this our President has just declared opioid abuse a national emergency and vows to help curb both the distribution and production of addictive and dangerous drugs. It is going to take everyone coming together to work on this problem, but I am glad to see the spotlight on this terrible epidemic.

Personally, I think legalizing marijuana is a bad idea and I think time will prove it. The debate on legalizing it has grown more difficult as more states have now passed legislation legalizing it. I'm flat out against teens doing **any** type of drugs and I think alcohol (also a drug) is just as bad as teens are drinking large volumes of straight alcohol. New information indicates that the age for trying marijuana is getting younger by the day. Many experts argue that marijuana is a "gateway" drug leading to other, harder drugs like heroin and cocaine. You don't have to look very hard to find current research on these facts. *As parents, we must do everything we can to encourage our kids to stay away from drugs and from heavy drinking.*

We Didn't Grow Up Like This:

If you have teens or especially grown children and grandchildren, you know that the majority of us didn't grow up this way. Back in my high school day, there was drinking going on but most were not binge drinking daily. Back in our day, there was only one type of vodka--not all these flavored kinds. I don't think I ever knew what a "shot" was until I got to college. Even then, I didn't feel compelled to "do shots." As adolescents' brains develop, heavy drinking and drugs alters cognitive development (for more, read "The Teenage Brain" by Dr. Jensen). The bottom line is that teens who abuse drugs and alcohol not only put others at risk (driving) but can permanently alter their brain development. Think about that! Ten years ago, we didn't have the science to support this. We do now, so if nothing else, tell your kids that if they want to be smart and be able to focus and have jobs when they grow up, they need their brains!

Who They Hang Out With:
I think it is critical to recognize bad influences on kids which--during the teen years--comes mostly in the form of peers. You must know who your kids are hanging out with and as they come home to talk to you about it (they are seeking advice whether or not they ask for it), we must have an open ear to listen. As parents we must LISTEN to our kids during this impressionable age. In middle school, our daughter would come home talking to us about other kids and their behavior. While she might not have specifically asked our opinion, we would listen to her and confirm she was right and support her feelings and thoughts. I think this was our way of saying "stay away from that girl" without having to use the words. Kids with sound value systems just need confirmation later and that's what we do as parents. Listening to her and agreeing with her was the validation she was seeking even if it was subconsciously.

More times than not, our house was the house where the kids all congregated. Not because they were having big parties, but because they were not. We were always home to feed them and my kids' friends always knew they were always welcome in my house (still are). I can remember times when I would tell Jim that we'd have to cancel our plans and stay home if kids were coming over. And we did. I thought that being at home with them was more important than anything else we had planned. Even if all you are doing is feeding them and keeping an eye out, they know you care. Kids want parents who care where they are and what they are doing because it means that they are loved and valued. By the time they reach 17, 18 hopefully--wherever they are (college, other people's houses, etc) they carry your values and love. I sometimes text mine this: "Remember where you came from" and I always tell them I love them--every, single day. And the reality is---sadly--that kids don't have enough wholesome outlets for entertainment. Crime has become such a deterrent to kids seeking "something fun to do" on weekends. I'd rather have them at my house eating pizza and watching movies than roaming the mall or hanging out in a random parking lot.

When you become a parent that other kids will talk to, you can also become a valuable mentor. They may not talk to their own parents but they might talk to you. Our kids sometimes had friends whose parents didn't seem to care where they were. Some had parents who were divorced and sometimes used the kids for leverage, often putting them in the middle or uncomfortable spots. You never know what is going on in the complicated life of kids, but we must love them and protect them because we have no replacements. I tell my kids and their friends often that "I love all my children" and I do. I treat them like my own too--even washed a few mouths out with squeeze soap when needed. "Mama Howell" some call me. A badge of honor in my book! Thankfully, now many of these kids are over 21 and I'm still enjoying them and still telling them what I think--whether they ask for it or not. We never stop being parents, right? Just last week I had a chat with one of our son's friends about his career. He brought it up and we just listened and then told him what we thought and that he was doing the right thing. Good stuff. Important stuff.

I remember talking to a friend, the dad of three really good grown kids when ours were younger. I asked him what the secret was to raising such great kids and he said something like "once you know they have your values, our job is like a pinball machine--we just keep them from going into those holes...you just bounce them back in the right direction." So we are like those little rubber flaps that you hit and we keep them going. I have never forgotten that! Pretty good, actually. Rubber bouncing flappers, we are.

Here is my best advice I can give you from my own parenting experiences and being around other parents who hold the same values.

- Just say NO: While I like the idea behind this campaign, I have always thought that explaining the **why** behind the **no** is the extra step--the most important one. It's easy to say "because I said no." The harder parenting requires going into why you are saying no and what the logic is behind it. We have told our kids that drugs are a dead end street and if they want a high gear life, they steer clear of them and those friends who do drugs. We believe in a zero tolerance when it comes to drugs and schools that drug test are doing themselves and parents a big favor by doing so--not because it actually works for the kids who do drugs but it gives those who don't want to an excuse not to
- We support drug testing: If your kids know they'll be tested, they have a great excuse to fight peer pressure. Schools should drug test and so should sports teams. Our kids need legitimate and positive reasons to fight peer pressure and we need institutions and leaders with the backbone to stand up for what is right for our kids
- Keep them busy: I know I said earlier that kids can be overscheduled but keeping kids busy and productive is different and helpful. Our kids had jobs in high school in addition to doing a sport and keeping up with homework. Jobs teach kids responsibility and help channel kids to be more productive with their spare time (since they have none)
- Grandparents influence: Thankfully, our kids have had good grandparent interaction and quality time with them. If you think we are strict, try my parents--that generation was, in my opinion, very strict and some of this is a good thing for teens these days
- Faith and church: joining a youth group and a church is a great way for kids to connect, share and get mentoring; Our kids went on some of the summer youth group church camps and we think

those are critical to keeping kids away from drugs and people who do them
- Don't be too strict: Well this is a tightrope to walk I know but it's true for our family. We all know people with ultra-strict parents and what happens is the kids never learn how to adapt when they leave the nest. We must teach our kids how to handle drinking while they are under our roof. We don't condone drinking under the legal age but we don't shy away from letting them have a glass of wine at the Christmas table or a beer in a fishing boat--sometimes with my parents present. Back in our day, the legal drinking age was 18 and I think that is a good thing. I think we should get back to spending quality time with our families and teaching them responsible, social guidelines. Most kids are going to find a way to drink anyway and wouldn't you rather be with them and be able to guide them? We need to teach our kids what is responsible and what is not. I'm sure some parents may disagree and that is fine. We should be comfortable having the dialogue. What is right for my family may not be right for another. I think it also GREATLY depends on your child. If they have that addictive gene, if they are mentally unstable, if they have tendency to disobey parents, other behavior issues, etc. then it might be that a different path is needed. If so, get professional help
- Be tough when you need to: You are the parent, not the pal: We were consistently tough on our kids when they were young and as they grew older, we didn't have to be. One day my daughter said I was mean and I said, "yes, and I can be meaner." Kids need boundaries and gain a better sense of direction when parents enforce the rules consistently
- Good parenting requires time with your kids: You only have about 14 years to spend quality time with your kids during the formative years. Spend as much time with them as you can and schedule time if you have to. If you work--like we all have to--put your kids first in front of social events and make sure you do everything you can to

invest your time in them. It will pay dividends later and kids who have more family time tend to steer away from drugs.
- Take your kids to the morgue: I'm serious. Arrange to take them to see a cadaver or two of teens who have died from drug abuse. The impression it makes and the evidence that kids do actually die, is lasting. In Memphis we have a gem called the MERI (Medical Education Research Institute) and they do medical research on cadavers donated to the organization. Part of their community outreach includes school tours and kids can see the morgue and cadavers of those who have been killed in car accidents, etc. It makes an impression on the teen brain as many have never seen a dead body. Shocking, yes, but if it can prevent a death, it's worth the shock. Unfortunately, many kids have seen friends die of car wrecks and/or drug related accidents and this is just tragic on many levels
- Seek counseling, therapy, rehabilitation if your kid is addicted to drugs or alcohol. It is a chemical dependency--a medical issue. Most parents would never deprive their kids from medical attention for a broken bone. Chemical addiction requires medical intervention from a trained expert.

About Teen Drinking:

I won't sugarcoat it: they drink. Even the "high gear" achievers are drinking. Not all of them of course, but many if not most. The differences from when we grew up are a few and I'd like to share that here. And parents, if you are reading this, I encourage you to share this with your kids and use it to have a discussion.

- New Science: The adolescent brain is not fully developed until the age of 25. We didn't know that--based on science--until very recently. Excessive alcohol can permanently damage the brains of developing teens. If you want to really understand this, I urge you to purchase and read the book, "The Teenage Brain," by Dr. Frances E. Jensen (M.D. mother and Neuroscientist) and Amy Ellis Nutt. The book factually describes evidence on how drugs and alcohol (and their combination) impact the teen brain--permanently. Here is one paragraph from the book that summarizes it well: *"Because of the flexibility and growth of the brain (during this time), adolescents have a window of opportunity with an increased capacity for remarkable accomplishments. But flexibility, growth and exuberance are a double-edged sword because and 'open' and excitable brain also can be adversely affected by stress, drugs, chemical substances, and any number of changes in the environment. And because of an adolescent's often overactive brain, those influences can result in problems dramatically more serious than they are for adults." (Page 23, "The Teenage Brain)*. So what Dr. Jensen is saying is that their brains are literally sponges and substance abuse can permanently impact their future brain development (read her book!!!).

- They are drinking MORE: Back in our day, we drank (legally at 18) but I recall heavy drinking being more the exception than the rule. Most of our college drinking involved beer and most of it on campus (we didn't have to leave and drive). Today kids are doing many shots--so many that alcohol poisoning is becoming more common and teens are dying in hospital emergency rooms. Robert Stutman gave us the stats on how many college kids arrive in the ER's daily across the USA. Some make it (if they get there in time) and many die. The numbers are real and terrifying.

- Focus on PARTY at the College level: All you have to do is watch the "Spring Breaks" of today and see how the drinking has changed. Also, the total lack of remorse. In our day, drinking too much was frowned upon and we felt a nice heap of guilt that went along with that headache. Today it's like a badge of honor and that must change. Where have we gone wrong? Why aren't adults and colleges saying "too much is too much" and if they are, why aren't our kids more aware of these dangers? We can't stop our kids from drinking but we can teach them the SCIENCE behind how too much will permanently limit them--or worse, kill them! Our colleges, teachers, mentors, advisors--and all of us--need to do a better job on this issue of excessive partying in college.

- Society focus on drinking and partying: If CNN can show on live television their adult reporters drinking and holding marijuana pipes (on New Year's Eve) what message are we sending our kids? We had all better be highly concerned about how our culture is shaping and influencing our kids.

For more on this, read Jensen's book and also look up the statistics that Robert Stutman provides. He is a great resource, speaker and communicator on this topic.

So as parents, what do we do about this excessive drinking? We have (I pray) talked to our kids about it and unfortunately, have had some of their friends have problems with alcohol which has led to even more conversation at our house. We have had some not so pleasant experiences which we have tried to use as teaching opportunities. We have to--all of us--teach our kids the limitations and dangers of too much alcohol and "binge drinking." When kids are dying and we know it, we must have conversations and help our kids get it so that they don't put themselves or anyone else in danger.

We need more leaders, mentors and role models for young kids that will step up and have the courage to speak out. I am personally sick of the political correctness in our country and I think we are doing our kids a big disservice by not saying what needs to be said for fear of offending them. When we allow halftime shows at national college football championship games that feature vulgar acts and vulgar lyrics displayed on national television for all to see, we are encouraging a culture that accepts that as the "norm." We have become so "politically correct" and so "open minded" that our brains are falling out. Our kids are looking for adult leadership that embraces strong ethical values and integrity. Watching a rapper grab his crotch and "sing" such vulgar lyrics is unacceptable in such a venue (in my opinion, anywhere for that matter). I'm not against freedom of expression, but there's a time and a place for such things and I don't think national television where families are watching is the place for it. Why do we let people who grab their privates in public in the name of entertainment have the stage? If ESPN was responsible for that talent booking, somebody should have their head examined. I don't care if you are liberal, conservative, white, black or purple: there is no excuse for condoning and promoting vulgarity on a national stage for all to see. There is a difference between right and wrong and we need to stand up for what is right and reject what is wrong as parents. What worries me is that a lot of people said they changed the channel at halftime. That's one way to limit what our kids see, but that's like putting a band-aid on cancer. We need to stop all of that in the first place. And it's all about money so, we need strong leaders to stand up to this type of behavior. We need people in positions of influence to have the backbone to say, "hey, this isn't right, let's find another way." Our kids deserve better.

I also think personally, that we should consider making the legal drinking age 18 again so we can help our kids figure it out before they flee the nest. We need to do something because what we have now is clearly not working. And I don't know the answer to this but my guess would be that 80% (maybe higher) of all kids around the age of 18 have fake identification. These fake i.d. Driver's license cards are apparently easy to obtain. So yes, our kids are already drinking at 18. Wouldn't it be better if we were honest about it? Is sneaking into bars and drinking illegally anyway while trying to hide it from parents the right experience? I don't think so. Wouldn't it be better if our kids could legally drink at 18 and then we could have experiences and honest conversation that are helpful and constructive? I think by restricting them to 21, we are putting them at greater risk.

I think exposing our kids to healthy options, smart people and those in influential careers who know the perils of drugs and alcohol are good strategies. Medical professionals, EMT's, pilots, police--all of these people would be good resources for mentoring our kids on this topic. In conclusion here, we know that raising the drinking age and telling kids not to do it hasn't worked. We must find stronger, more influential ways to guide our kids along this slippery slope.

When Bad things Happen in Families:
Growing up with a father who was the senior pastor at large churches in the south, yes, bad things happen in families. Fortunately for me and my siblings, not much really bad happened to my family. My parents argued some (like most do), but nothing out of the norm of most healthy families. I never heard them threaten divorce, they provided a safe and loving home and gave us that security kids need in order to thrive. However, others around us experienced drug and alcohol abuse, overdoses, insecurity issues that led to suicides, divorces, kids shipped away to boarding schools, and on and on. Most families go through hard times at some point or another. If you haven't, you can count yourself in the fortunate minority.

Our family has been tested recently with a medical crisis that rocked our lives, disrupted our stable lifestyle, and has challenged all of us in ways we could never imagine. We have made it through the medical crisis but not all of the financial, emotional impact of going through a hell I wouldn't wish on my worst enemy. The damage a big medical crisis can do to a family is unlimited. It could have broken us--our family, our marriage, our very lives. Instead, our kids stepped up big time. They leaned heavily on their key values. They made choices and sacrifices for the family. They saw more than any kids should ever have to see parents endure. Death would have been easier (not better, easier). Our kids passed a test of a lifetime with flying colors and you cannot imagine how that makes my heart sing! But it has been with both heartache and joy to watch my kids handle this crisis. Our "coping mechanisms" kicked into high gear--we drew strength from our solid values, foundational faith-based life, good friends and a sheer will of not giving in or up. During the crisis, I rallied my tribe of support and prayed that God would lead me through the wilderness where I found direction and strength to get us all through it. Sometimes I felt as though I was one with the wilderness and was just praying I didn't get devoured by it. Some days I felt like I was having out of body experiences, the ordeal was just beyond my imagination. More about this journey in my 3rd book, "Healing in High Gear." Bottom line: that which does not kill you makes you stronger if you can view it this way and keep moving.

And here's something else about a real life crisis. When your kids have to step up and act like adults, they can either sink or swim. This all happened during Bryan's senior year in high school. We couldn't tour colleges. We could hardly find time to apply to any. Bryan was accepted into Mississippi State but opted for University of Memphis instead. At a time when he should be leaving the nest and focusing on his own life of college--and the excitement that goes with it--he knew he couldn't. For several reasons. His dad was deathly sick. Our financial picture had drastically changed. We needed him. Abby was just starting high school and Bryan knew that by attending college in Memphis, he could help hold our family together. Bryan--then at age 18--had stepped up to be the man he is. He helped me pay bills and find things on Jim's computer. He helped me with all of the house chores and a lot of the things that Jim was not there to do. I will never forget it and we tell him often how proud he makes us. Currently, he's happy about being a junior at the University of Memphis, has a job and is doing well. Every family must do what is right for their situation. I tell my kids often that it's not what happens to you, but how you handle what happens.

Abby also stepped up in big ways as did her friends. She didn't give me one ounce of trouble. In a time when--at age 15--she could have rebelled and given me trouble, she did just the opposite. She got her hardship driver's license and joined the team Howell to help with Jim's recovery. She did well in school despite being on an emotional rollercoaster. This included spending many late nights at the hospital, often fending for herself at dinner, catching rides to school, never complaining, doing her laundry and in general, being a force of positivity and faith in our family. Her positive attitude and willingness to do whatever it took amazed me. You never know how good parenting will pay off until you are truly tested. Blessings!

About High School:

"Dear God, deliver me from the days of high school and get my kids through it alive."

That is literally the prayer I prayed, daily while my kids were in high school. High school is when all of your parenting pays off, is challenged and when you really need to be on your A-game as a parent. First--and most horribly--they are driving. Second, equally as disturbing--they are dating. You might as well plan on staying in top physical shape and the sleep deprived nights you had when they were newborns comes back as they push curfew limits and keep you awake at night worrying. Even the best kids will have nights when something goes awry. I can give you some examples here in a list:

- They are on their way home in a pouring down rainstorm ten minutes before a midnight curfew and someone runs a red light and t-bones their car: be grateful if nobody is hurt. You jump out of bed when you get the call and go to the scene of the wreck where you deal with the police and other driver--for hours. Lucky if everyone is okay and you get to bed by 3 a.m.;
- The plan changes minute by minute. First, they are going to sleep over at Amanda's house. Whoops, you get a text at about 11 p.m. that they are going to Hannah's house. We learned that if that started happening, our rule was to order the teen straight home. As a top police officer told me once, "nothing good happens after midnight"--wise counsel;
- You find beer cans in a closet: it will happen if you have high school kids in and out of your house. We used this as dinner table conversation and to their credit, our kids always told us the truth about how the beer cans got there. It didn't happen a lot, but it does happen.
- The friends have more ideas than they do brain cells: You train your kids and as soon as they start driving in high school, all these new kids appear with all kinds of new ideas for your kids. Stay calm and carry a firearm if you have to. I'm kidding here but you have to sometimes put the hammer down--especially in high school;
- A kid who is spending the night under your roof decides to sneak out and drive home at 3 or 4 a.m. Not cool, but it happens. Those kids are usually not invited back to our home;
- You get a call while you are at a nice dinner with friends that they need you to come pick them up right now--you do it of course. My suggestion is to go eat early so if you do get that call, you don't have to flush a nice dinner down the drain;

- They tell you they are going to a "concert" and you assume it's in town. Don't laugh but we assumed our kid was attending a country music concert at the nearby venue only to learn later they were all at a concert in another state--ask specific questions;
- You get a call that someone had a fight/breakup or problem and now 6 kids are coming over at curfew to spend the night and would it be possible to order several pizzas--we always said yes.

I'm sure there are more examples that many have. My point is that high school years are complicated by the fact that they are driving and they are around so many other people who influence them. Combine those with raging hormones and an underdeveloped brain. This is a natural and frightening to most parents. Unfortunately things are so different now than they were when we grew up, but that doesn't mean your values are any different. We have tried to raise our kids mostly the way we were raised. High school is a big challenge and where all your parenting skills will be fully tested--and I mean *fully*. Be the parent, not the pal.

About them having jobs and debit cards:

I was having dinner last night with a client and his wife who have three good kids ages 17, 14 and 10. While at dinner my client got a text that he needed to deposit money into the 17-year old's account for something they needed to purchase. Sound familiar? I had to laugh because we get these text messages too. In this digital world of banking now we can transfer money on our phones while we are out having dinner.

I have already mentioned the benefits a job can give your driving teen. Not only do they have to work for someone and have a boss (who isn't you the parent) but they will earn a paycheck and will have to put it in the bank. I recommend a joint bank account with a debit card in your child's name that you also have access to. We did this for both of our kids when they started working and driving. Our kids are tech-savvy and they can download the banking app and check their balances which they do often. This teaches them how to manage their own money while still in high school which will be a huge advantage once they are in college. It is much easier to help them figure all of this out while they still live at home. By the time they get to college, they'll have had a debit card for a few years so they know how to use it and manage it.

We love our kids having jobs. Once our daughter had to stop running cross country due to a foot injury, she got a job hostessing and assisting servers at a local restaurant. She has had this job now for almost two years and will start waiting tables in a few months as she turns 18. She earns her own spending money and has learned to manage her bank account. She shops sales and watches her spending closely. Her job skills will be transferable anywhere she goes and working in a fine dining establishment has taught her a lot about real life. She's had to deal with customers, clean tables, set tables, assist the waiters, fetch waters, clean silverware, hostess, answer the phone and much more. The absolute best part about her job (besides earning her money) is that she has a boss that's not me.

While in high school, our son had a job at a local community center where he lifeguarded year round and taught swim lessons (the stories he told us about some of the kids and their parents had me crying laughing so hard). Later, in college, he got a part-time job working afternoons after class in a warehouse operating a forklift and unloading/loading freight (thank you Carrie Sellers). He has had to learn the balance of getting his class work done, maintaining his GPA to keep his scholarship and working sometimes 30 hours per week. He pays for his own gas, internet, hobbies, some of the expenses of his housing and anything else he wants to in his spare time. Fortunately for him, we pay for his college tuition, his rent, his insurance, his books and we give him a small monthly amount for some of his food. It's not much so somehow he has made it work. There are days when he only has $2 in his debit account but he doesn't go into overdraft. And even better, he doesn't ask us for more money. Instead, he works his job(s) to earn that money. It's what we call having "skin in the game" and important for kids to learn early.

No matter what happens, try and avoid agreeing to and signing off on a credit card for your kid. Credit cards should be avoided if possible as debt becomes a real anchor for kids (and anyone). I realize there are times when people need credit cards, but I would avoid it if possible. Being in debt is a challenging way to start a life of independence. Our kids are faced with enough challenges already and we should try and do everything possible to help them stay out of debt (and teach them about debt). A lot of college graduates are having to move back in with their parents due to having to pay off loans and debt. They don't earn enough in their jobs to pay their own rent and manage debt at the same time.

I am glad that financial independence is coming for our kids. As parents, we all hope and pray that our kids will graduate from college, join the workforce and get off our payroll. We think kids who have jobs in high school and college have an advantage and have already had a head start on managing expenses. And the truth of it all is that many kids--including ours--have to work. Many parents cannot afford the full price tag associated with higher education and that is why saving for college when your kids are babies is so important.

About buying them cars:

When they start driving, most parents are faced with what to do about buying their kids cars. We certainly don't want them driving our cars, so my advice is to get something well used and fairly safe (large) because I'm here to tell you, they are going to wreck them. And boys like to add things to cars like light bars, HD lights and other things that end up costing you repairs. Boys who try and wire their own cars with whatever they are adding often do it wrong so just a heads up on that speaking from experience. Boys also think it is fun to go mudding off road and are more apt to have tire damage and other damage to cars or trucks. Most girls don't do this. Abby has never felt compelled to take her car mudding or winch someone out of a ditch. Abby has, however, learned the art of using jumper cables and Bryan has learned (we hope) to check the oil.

Giving your kids a new car--no matter how good their grades are--is flushing your money down the drain. For one thing, the insurance will be higher. For another thing, they need to work for those newer cars. Instead, buy them a car that already has some wear and tear on it because they will hit a mailbox, rear end someone, back into a tree, and get t-boned by a driver who runs a red light. They also go places where they park too close to others and park near other teens. Have you been to a high school parking lot at 3:00 in the afternoon? Girls are driving while looking at their phones and talking and boys aren't even looking where they are going. It's truly scary seeing teens drive and a wonder there aren't more accidents.

When Abby needed a car (and she had a job so we had no choice) we found an old hunter green Suzuki mini-suv like thing that Abby named "Chester." I think we paid $4,000 for it but it had new tires on it and ran okay. She drove it for a few years until we could upgrade to a 2004 "Wanda the Honda" CRV with 100,000 miles on it. We don't care if she gets door-dinged or bumps into a tree. And next year when she's at college, that car will be just fine sitting there on campus with thousands of other teen driven cars. Kids should be grateful they even get to have a car in my opinion. And many kids have to work to pay for their own cars which I think teaches them to appreciate what they have and to take care of what they have.

The Importance of Vo-Tech:
A vocational-technical school (often called "Vo-tech school) in high school is critical to those kids who need an alternative route to successful employment in the future. While many kids don't get a college degree (for a variety of reasons), we need for them to learn skills and trades that can make them employable in the workforce. Many of these skilled workers perform jobs that earn high wages which is important. I think kids need to learn to work with their hands and learn how to build things and repair things. Back in the day, we had more vo-tech and classes like "shop" (machine repair) and even home economics. We need to bring this back for our kids!

CHAPTER 5

7 Nights at the Dinner Table: The Decline of Family Activities

"All great change in America begins at the dinner table."
--Ronald Reagan

It's hard to imagine growing up eating dinner at the dinner table every night with parents but we did. It was rare that we did not and sadly, today, that is reversed. In our world now, it is rare that kids eat dinner with the family--all at the same time around the table. Sports, school activities, work, all drive a wedge between family members spending time together regularly.

As a new parent, you are bonding with your newborn through regular routines and being home to physically take care of their needs. As children grow and become more independent, we stray from those routines and we are all guilty of it.

As older parents of grown and almost grown good kids, we have certainly struggled in the day to day challenges of family together time, but we placed a value on it. Our value to put family first is what drove us to work hard to try and carve out that time for our families to be together.

I remember as a teen in Mobile, AL, I loved Wednesdays because we got to eat at the church and our church had an incredible cook. Every other night, my mom cooked mostly and--although she was a good cook--sometimes we didn't love what was "on the menu" at our house. I was raised to eat what was served or not eat. Today, kids are so spoiled with options, fast foods and technology that allows you to have what you want when you want it. Uber Eats--whatever you want delivered right to your door.

It's really not about the food as much as it's about the experience. Every single time I serve a meal at our table, we linger longer, talk more and interact with our kids. It truly gets harder as they get older as schedules collide, but parents who try and make it a priority are doing themselves and their kids a big favor. If you work and cannot cook, pick up take-out and bring it home. Sometimes I serve fast food on paper plates around our table.

I have said earlier that I make our kids put the phones down at dinner and now it is just expected. When we gather around any table, the kids start telling us about things at school, and before we realize it, we have been there an hour or more! What's even better is if the grandparents join us and then the stories start and we could be at the table forever! That is what our families need more of and this is what kids crave. If nurturing a newborn is important to you, then nurturing your teen should be too. The dinner table is a great place to do it! Just look at the Italians. I love their culture and I love the big, family, long lunch and dinners at their tables with huge families. What great therapy for whatever ails us.

I have always loved being at a dinner table. We celebrate around one and isn't it so fun to set a great table? I just love seeing photos in magazines of long tables of 20 or more set for a celebration, sometimes even outside. It just brings a happiness to me and I think, "I'd love to be a guest at that table." One of my joys is to decorate a dinner table whether it's just fun paper plates or the finest china I have. I'll even polish silver goblets and sometimes surprise my guests or family with a formal and beautiful table. The joy for me is sharing it and making everyone around it feel welcome and comfortable. And the more the merrier! I love it especially when our kids ask if they can invite friends to join us. No matter if the table is already set, I'm always ready to "add more plates and chairs" at the drop of a text. I wish we'd get back to more time around the dinner tables! It truly is medicinal for families and I think kids who grow up having family dinners often benefit from it in ways they don't even realize.

Here are some of my tips and things we did that may be of use to your family:

- Make dinner easy--grab it and serve it on paper plates
- Tell your kids early in the day that you expect them at dinner at a certain time
- Try and have dinner at least 4 nights per week even if sports means it is late
- Go out to dinner if you can together; I know it's expensive but we often found places that didn't cost an arm and leg that our kids loved
- Don't make your kids clean up every time: if they think dinner at the table means work after that, they may resist (hence paper plates)
- Make them ask to be excused from dinner; We grew up having to ask and we have passed this very polite manner down to our own kids
- Pick a night that is "family night" and let the kids pick the menu; We did that in our family and when the kids were little I would let them

pick what I would cook. Dinner and then movie night was a great way to celebrate "family night"
- If you can't have dinner around the table, go for breakfast OR ice cream later: as our kids aged, just hanging out in our kitchen and talking became the norm: as they age, be present in whatever place they land! In the high school years we often had late night sandwiches or pizzas in our kitchen.
- Celebrate special events around the dinner table: birthdays, holidays, good report cards, awards, etc.
- Don't be too hard on yourself and make dinner fun: Kids are easy to please and I learned the hard way that a good box of mac-n-cheese or a pizza was better than slaving over something complicated out of a cookbook.
- Use a crock pot and look up the easy meals that cook while you are at work

I say all of this and it comes to mind that you must do this when they are in the pre-driving years. Once they drive, they may have jobs, sports, they have their own social lives and you are lucky if you can have 2 nights a week around the dinner table. Yes, the driver's license is the "crossing over" point for our kids so you must do this early! And as they get older and drive, parents must fight for a time to rally the family together. It is especially important as they face difficult challenges as teens. Probably even more important!

CHAPTER 6
Bullying, Peer Pressure & Jealousy

> *"The common mistake that bullies make is assuming that because someone is nice that he or she is weak. Those traits have nothing to do with each other. In fact, it takes considerable strength and character to be a good person."*
> --Mary Elizabeth Williams

You cannot raise kids these days without some type of brush up with peer pressure and bullying. Two different things but they certainly seem to go hand in hand. When teens are committing suicide at alarming rates in our society, you know that it is a big problem. And there is a big difference between "fighting" and bullying. Though we as parents discourage solving problems by fighting--sometimes it happens. Bullying is real and we need to do everything we can to stop it when we can.

Home should be where kids and families feel loved and safe. Unfortunately too many of our kids are not safe at home and that is a huge tragedy. Tragically, many kids are physically, emotionally, sexually and mentally abused in their own homes. Kudos to the social workers, non-profits and champions of kids out there doing work to try and help these kids. We must keep trying and never give up!

Loving homes provide security and a place for kids to grow and thrive. When you are loved at home--no matter what you did or no matter what goofy clothes you insisted on wearing--kids do better. Home should be a place where kids are protected and accepted for who they are. Our love for our kids (and others) teaches them to love others. I was fortunate to grow up in a very loving, supportive home. Giving your kids a positive, encouraging home environment is critical to raising good kids, I believe. Parents who bully their own kids shouldn't have had any, in my opinion.

Parents, don't bully your kids about sports performances, beauty contests or being overweight. Don't talk about how bad their hair might look or how they need to shave. Don't put them down or criticize them. As a parent, our job is to be their biggest fan, cheerleader and avid supporter in life. Even when I notice my son's hair getting too long, I try and avoid saying anything. Kids go through "phases" of things like having long hair. While it may bother you some, try to ignore it. Remember that kids are developing their self-esteem and self worth. Be a positive part of that by loving and supporting them at each stage. They'll eventually get a haircut.

What truly matters is what is on the inside of someone. I remember when our daughter was younger she hadn't hit her growth spurt yet and was sporting a few extra pounds. I never thought much about it, but to this day she looks back at photos and calls it her "fat stage." I always respond by saying she wasn't fat and that it didn't matter anyway. Society puts a big price on kids--girls especially--to look perfect and be thin. We always steered away from that and told our kids that people come in all shapes and sizes. It's also important to teach kids not to make fun of those who don't conform to mandates of style magazine editors in a society that worships beauty and physical perfection.

Looking back on my own experience, I remember being bullied at school and it was not fun. I was able to resolve my own problems but sometimes it took creativity. When I was a freshman in high school--a rough, public high school--I had a bully who threatened bodily harm to me everyday until some of my friends put a stop to it. Now those of you wanting to guess my age, I will tell you back in the day, we were wearing "Candies" (although admittedly nobody could really walk in them) and rocking out to songs like "Call Me" by Blondie, "Upside Down" by Dianna Ross and "Coming Up" by Paul McCartney. We were wearing our hair "big" with "feathers" inspired by the late Farrah Fawcett --one of our then aspire-to-be-like celebs. Some of us were sleeping in pink sponge rollers and wearing "training bras" and shoulder pads. We were driving old, beat up cars (if we were even lucky to have one) and talking only on land lines with no internet. And we loved our high school football team. It was the late 70's/early 80's.

Now this bully was female and had targeted me for some unknown reason to me. She was not in any of my classes but would threaten me in the hallway and during our lunch wave. She would shove me into the lockers and tried pushing me down the stairs at several points. I did try once to talk to her which ended up in several of her friends wanting a fight. I just walked away--scared to death that fight was surely coming.

One day, a male friend of mine (with known connections to some tough drug dealers in our school) asked me about it. I told him I didn't know why she had zeroed in on me and that I hadn't done anything that I knew of to make her feel the way she did. My male friend witnessed her threat to me one day and asked if he and his friends could take care of her. I asked what "take care of her" meant and he just said they'd have a talk with her. I made him promise me that he would not let anyone physically hurt her. The next day after school was over, several of his friends followed her to her car and had some type of conversation with her and she never even looked my direction again. I don't know what they said and I didn't want to know but she never bothered me again. That was one day I knew what it must be like to have a big brother. Since I didn't actually have one, it was nice to have male friends who would take up for me.

Thankfully, I had friends in high school from all walks of life, but most of my high school friends had parents like mine so my circle of friends stayed out of trouble for the most part. Going to a public school really opened my eyes to what drugs could do and we also witnessed violence on our campus almost daily. I remember one student dying after being stabbed multiple times in a knife fight. The school got much better as a new principal had arrived who put a stop to a lot of the bad stuff going on. Being in that type of environment is both stressful and educational--not just academics but amping up your "street smart" game. I steered clear of drugs and focused my high gear on doing well in high school which ended up landing me a full scholarship to the University of Alabama as well as an acceptance to Rhodes College.

Our kids have not been the targets much of bullies but they have seen others who have. They have stuck up for their friends and stood up to some bullies. Sadly, they have seen suicides in middle school where bullying may have played a role. Unfortunately, our school systems are not equipped to handle the volume of bullying that takes place. Technology has now enabled "cyber bullying" which can be just as bad if not worse. Parents must use every arrow in their quiver to help kids deal with bullies.

One day, Abby was riding home on the school bus and had won a prize from the school treasure chest so she selected a whoopi-cushion that made a loud farting sound when you sat on it (Naturally, I would have picked the same thing). The bus driver didn't like it. In fact, she didn't like kids much either. I was outside in our yard cutting grass when Abby got off the bus with tears streaming down her little precious face (she was maybe 6). Alarmed, I stopped the mower and went to her while the bus driver rudely drove away giving me "the look." Abby told us that the bus driver had been mean to her and had shut the door on her when she tried to get off the bus. Completely unacceptable and downright bullying a kid. Can you imagine having those big bus doors shut on a 6 year old?

What the bus driver didn't realize is that I had a secret weapon in store for her: our nanny, Ruthie. And we loved her and she loved "her Abby." So when all this happened, I said "I'm going to have a chat with that bus driver when she comes to pick up Abby in the morning." Immediately Ruthie said, "Oh no you won't. I will be the one to do it. You let a black woman talk to a black woman." I'll admit I was sort of surprised by Ruthie's statement but I thought about it and decided she was right. Sure enough, the next morning Ruthie (one of the stars in my first book, "Women in High Gear") and Abby were waiting for the bus driver. I was inside where I was told to stay watching like "Gladys Cravitz" out the window. After some words (Ruthie asked the bus driver if she liked her job and wanted to keep it), Abby got on the bus. I was worried the bus driver would take what Ruthie said out on Abby but she didn't. In fact, the bus driver never gave Abby one minute of her crap after that. Bus drivers can be bullies too!

Peer pressure can be--in my opinion--another form of bullying. The pressure on kids by their peers (and sometimes their own parents) to conform to whatever is "cool" or "in" or whatever the term is these days, is crazy. As parents, we constantly told our kids to "think for themselves" and to stay away from other kids who didn't share the same values. Remember in the earlier chapter about the importance of your value system? These come in handy when you are a teen. You must lean on those values for support in times of pressure.

Common things we have seen indirectly while parenting our teens: pressure to be independent too fast, pressure to drink, pressure to have sex, pressure to do drugs, pressure to resist authority, pressure not to like a certain person (mostly true with girls), pressure from "mean girls"--they do exist. Our kids have not had problems dealing with these things, but they have told us about it from time to time. At this phase, listening to them and letting them tell us is how we handled much of it. Those dinners around the table are when you hear about it. As parents, we listen, ask questions and support them as they sort it out. Often times our kids would tell us things I think for verification that they did the right thing. Praise your kids when they tell you how they handled something well and reinforce those key values with every experience. Kids learn by doing (don't we all?) and sorting out issues for themselves is important.

Parents who put too much pressure on their kids are doing themselves and their kids a big disservice. I have seen it first hand. I don't understand what parents think will be good about pushing and pressuring their kids. Is it because they want to re-live their own lives differently? I think most who do it think they are doing the right thing for their kids but they aren't, in my opinion.

I remember when our son, Bryan was in the 6th grade and had made some friends on the football team. One of the other mothers would take her son to school, park the car and carry all of his equipment for him all the way into the school. I sometimes watched this from my car after dropping Bryan off.

She would also drop everything to take something to the school if he forgot it or needed anything. One day my phone rang and it was her on the line crying about something that had occurred in the boys' locker room. Immediately concerned, I asked, "Oh my word, what happened?" Part of me was genuinely concerned while the other part was flat curious after all of my observations. She was so upset that she had difficulty getting the words out to tell me that all the boys had decided to have a "show and tell" to see who had the biggest penis. She felt they were bullying her son. Torn between wanting to laugh or help, I took a deep breath and told her I thought that boys did stuff like that and that as long as it was consensual, I wouldn't think it was bullying. I asked her if her son was hurt or upset by it and she said he wasn't but that she was. After trying to reassure her this was not a big deal--in my opinion--we finally hung up. I don't think I comforted her but as I hung up the phone I thought to myself "not there's a mom who is way too involved in her son's middle school life."

Boys will be boys and if you carry their equipment, baby and pamper them, and insert yourself into what they are doing in the locker room, you are not helping them. In fact, parents who get too involved and try to protect their kids too much often set the kids up to be bullied. It's why your son doesn't need you walking him inside to school after about the third grade. It's why they'd rather you drop them off 100 feet from the movie theatre door. They are needing to practice that independence and as parents, we need to let them! There is a balance of knowing when and how to help our kids and when to let them handle things.

Another example I'll share is when Bryan played baseball--a sport he liked okay but eventually decided to quit it (and we were fine with that). We were on a "recreation team"--not a competitive team so it's even worse that the parents acted out so badly! We had one father on the team who would yell so loud at the coach, the referees and other parents if things didn't go right for his son. It was so embarrassing and especially, I think for his son. His son wasn't that good (ours either) and it was a pure example of adding insult to injury for the poor kid. At 12 years old, you are supposed to be having fun! So some parents bully their own kids over sports! Unfortunately, our society (and schools are partly to blame) has placed such an important priority on competitive sports for kids that some parents are living the life they didn't through their own kids. I hear about it everyday and we saw it ourselves. When Bryan told us he'd rather not play baseball, half of me was thrilled because we got our weekends back and the other half of me was thrilled because I wouldn't have to listen to parents behaving badly.

Parents who think their kids need to be perfect and excel at every turn are probably in for a few surprises later. In our experience with our own kids, there comes a time when you have to step back and let them be. That doesn't mean you stop parenting. It means you take the baby bird and shove it out of the nest so it can fly. You are still there to protect and assist, but at some point--when they head to college--you have to let them go out into that world knowing that everything meaningful you taught them they likely learned by age 7.

At the point of me writing this, our son is now 21 and a junior in college. Although we are interested in his grades, we don't hover over him (he lives close to the campus with two roommates) and we don't ask him much about grades as he knows we expect him to do well. We don't call him to check on what time he's getting home and we don't really have to do much parenting at this point. We are more like an ATM and a place to land now and then for a home cooked meal and a tank of gas! The parenting tips we give him now are more about saving money, getting jobs, doing internships, networking and staying on track in school. By that, we mean embracing the curriculum, getting enough hours and graduating on time. He knows that after that comes a job and real life. School is a stepping stone in that process.

Our daughter is finishing high school and has steered away from "mean girls" and pressure. We don't worry about her much when it comes to peer pressure or bullying (We do however worry constantly about her safety in general). She has a good big brother who would insert himself if needed. I should say here that siblings can be a great source of help to teens when it comes to being bullied. Our son is almost 4 years older than our daughter and has been a huge help to us in certain situations. They have a great relationship and love one another fiercely. I think girls with big brothers are fortunate in many ways. They understand boys better and we always had a pack of boys around our house. Those boys are all like her brothers and I think there is security and comfort that comes in having big brothers (even though they fight and drive you crazy when they are young). A big brother or sister can be a stabilizing force in turbulent times. I will admit that our son would often have more influence on our daughter in certain situations. She would listen to him sometimes when she didn't want to listen to us. We also taught our son to value, respect and help protect women--something our society needs more of.

It is tempting, at times, to want to use one child to influence another. You parents out there reading this may clearly understand what I am saying. As Bryan grew up, sometimes I would catch myself telling him to influence Abby if he could one way or another. As parents, we have to resist that to some degree. While a sibling can be influential, it is not fair to pressure them to act like a parent. It's not right to put your kids in the position that you the parent should be in--and it's an easy habit to depend on older siblings. Try and avoid doing it and try and be mindful of it. Older siblings can be helpful but applying pressure on them to be a substitute for a parent is not fair to them, and may backfire as they may resent it and retaliate later.

Here are some tips for helping kids fight off bullies and peer pressure:

- Teach them early to think for themselves and hold onto those values
- Teach them self-defense and let them take courses for it
- Have a "family code" via a text message and a plan for intercepting your kids if they get into trouble (for example, if your kid sends a text that's one word code for 'come get me' you can then call the kid and say something like 'there has been a family emergency and I'm on my way to get you now' and the kid has a way out of a pressured situation)
- Let them share their locations with each other on their phones: our kids can locate us and each other on the GPS--a great safety feature
- Discourage bad behavior from other kids; Support your child's wishes to get away from mean kids and bullies
- Don't get involved in your kids' friendships unless it is an emergency; let them work it out and guard their privacy (don't talk to other parents about the kids unless it's urgent)
- Don't go to the school and talk to the teachers or administration without the approval and support from your child; Parents need to be more careful about inserting themselves into their kids' schools and lives at school: sometimes good intentions backfire and can create even more stress for your child at school
- Talk with your kids about your own bullies (past or present included) as they will listen to how you handle it
- Don't make your kids be friends with your friends' kids; Let them pick their own friends
- Report cyber stalkers or bullies to the authorities and educate your kids on the dangers of cyber stalking (ask a police officer to come talk to the school)

- Unfriend and unfollow (disengage) or block "mean girls" and bullies; I tell my kids if you cannot trust them, don't let them into your "cyber circles"

About siblings fighting:

I wanted to mention this here because we all know that as parents, our kids sometimes fight. They may fight one another often and sometimes they may fight with other kids. Some of this is normal, but we always encouraged our kids to settle differences without resorting to violence. Our kids seemed to fight when they were between the ages of 7 or 8 and 12 or 13. We never let our son hit or punch his sister (though I'm sure he did at times when we weren't in the same room) but I recall making them "take it outside." They would roll around "wrestling" on the playroom floor and when it got too rowdy, I would make them go outside. It's not as easy to roll around in grass, dirt, sticks with dogs jumping into the mayhem. Plus, I didn't want holes in my sheetrock or broken lamps. The main point I am making is that kids will fight and parents need to let kids work out their own problems when possible. Intervening too much (intervention is critical if there is truly someone hurting someone else) teaches kids they cannot problem solve on their own.

Our kids never really got into fights at school like we used to see back in the day. But there were times when we supported our kids if fighting was a last resort. I will not forget my husband telling our son that if some kid threw a punch first, sometimes you just have to answer it and make sure it's a harder punch. "If they hit you and don't look like they are going to stop, you make your best shot and hit with all you have," he said. Good advice and we would still support it. We live in a dangerous world and turning the other cheek is dangerous.

Boys are so different than girls!

As I write this, my daughter told me we had double standards for raising her as we let Bryan stay out later at night in high school. Guilty! We did. He could physically take care of himself so it is true. It's not just when it comes to their safety that boys are different. Girls and boys are way different when it comes to many things. As a parent, you should know this. You can read all the self-help books you want but experience is the best teacher. In our experience, girls are more mature, more observant (earlier), more discerning, more critical and definitely--at times--more work. Boys are happy as long as they are fed and have something to do--catch frogs, catch fish, kill a bird--at least that was the way it was in our home. Boys--when kept busy--were easy. You can pretty much live with boys by the general rule that they just want to eat, sleep and go outside. Girls--on the other hand--can break out in full meltdown mode with tears if they don't like the shirt they have on. And I hate to say this, but it is pretty much the same once they are older too. To this day, Abby cares way more about what she's wearing than her brother. Boys just don't seem to be bothered by small details. Except when it comes to their truck. Or their gun. Then, those details matter! All the men in my family deer hunt and I always tease them by saying they can spot a deer scrape in the woods but they cannot see the mud they are tracking all over my clean house.

Recently I was talking to the father of four kids. His first three are boys. His last is a girl. He said to me, "If we had had her first, we would have not had any more kids." He was telling me how much work she is and how the boys were so much easier.

Another key difference I'll mention as it relates to parenting is that girls will have more friends who "come and go" from their lives. Boys will just have a lot of friends. Don't worry about it and don't get too attached to some of your kids' friends. Girls--especially in high school--seem to have friends who one day are the "bff" and the next are not. I think some of this is normal but as parents we encourage our kids to be kind and not pile onto something if it is hurting someone. So I think relationship issues with girls are more complex than they are with boys. Boys do have relationships but they don't seem to have the drama--or investment in the relationship--that girls seem to have.

We feel fortunate to have had one of each so we have seen these differences firsthand. Not only in our kids but their friends as well. I laugh when I see moms and dads with three girls. And then I laugh when I see a mom or a dad with two boys. Boys are super busy all the time. In motion constantly. I remember when Bryan was a toddler (crawling) and I had to pull pots, pans and "stuff" out on my kitchen floor just to occupy him so I could cook dinner. With girls, you can pull out the dolls and they will sit still for hours. Boys don't care if they have mustard on their shirts. If a girl gets her shirt dirty, she's changing it. Boys love things that are gross--dead snakes (or anything dead) smelly farts and all of that gross stuff (do any of you parents remember that "fart spray" that came in the can and you could spray it in the air?).

Girls don't like this gross stuff. And by this I mean mostly. I know there are exceptions to all of this but in general, these are common observations. And boys just lay it all out there. One time I remember we were in Chick-fil-A and Bryan yelled out at the top of his lungs..."Mom, I have to POOOOOOOP!" The whole place laughed. I never recall Abby doing anything even remotely like that. Girls, however, can be more difficult later in life--as teenagers. Boys also become expensive as teenagers. Cars, repairs, cars, tires, repairs, cars... did I say cars? And one thing is for sure in our tribe: Girls eat just like boys AND they are just as messy as boys. Both of our kids rooms were a disaster zone on any given day. Just because girls have the ability to be neat and organized doesn't mean they will be. And I do know some men who tend to be super neat freaks. We don't have that gene in our family, sadly.

About Jealousy:
My mom and I have long said between the two of us that we think jealousy is the worst sin (it's actually not an act, but an emotion). If you Google it, you'll find similar threads of comments relating to being insecure, feeling envious or lacking something of personal value. Jealousy is described as an **emotion**. I think this is an important thing to include here in this book. I don't know if mean people are inherently jealous, but the older I get, the more I believe they are. I think jealousy is one of the most destructive of emotions, and as parents, we must teach our kids not to be jealous of others. Instead, we build great families and communities that are the opposite--supportive, loving and happy to see other people succeed. If you truly understand this, and can get your kids to as well, you are doing a great thing for them. Being happy for others and helping others succeed is what we need to be focusing on--as families, communities and our country. Sure, we all want success for ourselves but throwing darts and daggers at others to get what we want is not the way to do it.

We often see examples (in business and in politics, especially) where people are encouraged to do whatever it takes to get to the top. Cheat, steal, lie, stand on the shoulders of others, etc. If we can teach our children that this is wrong and really think about what jealousy does to people, we can set them ahead of the pack for life.

Jealousy is often at the heart of negativity. Jealous people-in my experience--are generally not happy. They will bully, be mean and often manipulate a situation to their advantage. Guard against jealousy. Nip it in the bud if you see it creeping into your children's relationships with others. It can start as easily as a child complaining that a friend has a better outfit or toy than they do. Stop right there and explain that there will always be people with "better stuff" but that it is our REACTION to it that counts.

When you are young parents, there is a temptation to try and keep up with what everyone else is doing (I guess this is true at any age, really). Try and avoid feeling jealous when you see your best friend buy a gorgeous new house with a pool that is about 100k more than you have to spend. It can be hard to live on a fixed income while others around you seem to grow money on trees in their yards. Put on your whole armour and guard against the evil of jealousy. It's a sneaky, slow creeper that wants to consume you but just don't let it. Instead, whip up a big batch of cookies and march over to your friend's new mansion and tell her how happy you are for her.

I have learned (the hard way sometimes) to steer clear of jealous people. I have worked with some and have watched them poison the well for others. Jealous people are not healthy influences for our kids. Sometimes it can take a few years for such jealousy to emerge, but watch for it and steer away from it. You may have heard the old saying "he doesn't have a jealous bone in his body"--those are the peeps I want to hang with!

One of my pet peeves as it relates to Facebook is people who make the comment they are "jealous" when others post things they are doing or trips they are on. I am amazed that people actually write "I'm jealous" in a comment as if that is something to be proud of. I deliberately make a habit of commenting in a positive way on people's pages. If I see a friend posting photos of a beautiful beach somewhere exotic, I will comment "Love this...keep the pics coming" or something positive like "I'm so glad you are on such a wonderful trip," (I do actually like looking at travel photos). The fact of the matter is that thankfully (kudos to my mom) I am not a jealous person. I don't understand that emotion but I do know it is destructive.

Practice the art of NOT being jealous by being happy for others. It becomes habit and I have actually told my kids that telling others you are happy for them is positive. When you hear a good kid say to another, "I'm happy for you," you know you have done a great job. Our daughter is especially genuinely happy to see others succeed. She is supportive of her friends and her non-selfish, non-jealous approach in relationships will be an asset to her all of her life.

CHAPTER 7
Social Media

> *"If we all work together there is no telling how we can change the world through the impact of promoting positivity online."*
> --GERMANY KENT

Some of this content has been covered in Chapter 3 but I want to expand on social media here. Snapchat, Facebook, You-Tube, Instagram....the list goes on and on and our children are on these platforms daily. Statistics support that teens watch more on YouTube than TV. Whether we like it or not, our world is now a digital, 24/7 social media news cycle and sometimes it can be overwhelming to us--especially teens. At the most vulnerable and impressionable time in their lives (when their brains are on overdrive neurologically) we have to deal with the pressures that come with too much information shared constantly. We believe we are headed into a time of "digital overload" and as parents, we think it is critical to recognize when our kids are too connected online and what to do about it. Our kids are overwhelmed with information yet they are starving for wisdom. Information alone is not wisdom and discernment. Our kids need guidance and wisdom from us as parents.

We aren't sure we know the answer as we all struggle as adults to find time to get things done. It requires focusing on the right priorities and intentionally making good choices. Personally, we think that Facebook has replaced a lot of "in real life" conversations. We think people rely on conversations online a lot rather than having them in person which can diminish the quality of the content being discussed as well as the overall tones. **Nothing digital replaces human interaction.** As parents, we must make sure our kids know this. There is no substitute for meeting someone, shaking his or her hand, looking them in the eye and having a conversation. It's also important to teach our kids civility and kindness. In our fast paced, digital world, we have lost the art of personal relationships. In this void of personal knowledge of each other, we jump to conclusions and often miss the mark about others.

If our kids don't master the true art and comfort of real life communication, they are not being equipped with life skills that are needed later for college interviews, jobs, etc. In our book "Students in High Gear" we address much of these important communication issues.

Social media is a tool (tools) that give us a platform for communicating in a viral way. It can give a small brand a big voice. Businesses and news outlets are now heavy users of social media and get much of their data from the online conversations. Everywhere you look--at any topic or debate--people are engaging online. However, the real benefit comes to those who take the online conversation into real life--actually meeting people face to face, getting to know that person, working on good networking in real life opportunities. I am a big believer in a powerful network in real life. Use social media to find people but then get to know them and meet them. It's hard to hate people once you know them. Wouldn't there be so much more positive human interaction if people really **knew** each other? Think about your own circle of friends and how it is easier to have a discussion with differing viewpoints. You respect them because you know that person. It's easier to "hate" online because people don't know each other. Your Twitter profile is not your complete persona. We really need to teach our kids to avoid hate dialogue online.

Instead, I advocate for using social media for good--harnessing the power of online engagement for positive outcomes. When channeled properly, social media can be a powerful force for good. But it doesn't replace human interaction where people talk and engage face to face.

But social media can be both a blessing and a curse. In my own experience I struggle with balancing posting content (both for myself, my brand and my clients') and finding that right rhythm for using it. I cannot imagine what our kids are going to be faced with ten years from now as this heavy "data everywhere" drives our lives. Much has been written about social media and digital and how brands and businesses are mining the data for improved products and strategies. Many of the new and emerging businesses are coming from technology and digital companies developing new applications and online offerings. It's overwhelming and impossible to keep up with.

Can you imagine how our kids feel? At their most impressionable stages, they are being bombarded by information, emerging technologies and constant keeping up of what is online. There is a documented real "fear of missing out" they experience if they cannot check their phones. I worry about what type of world we have created with all of this technology and wonder what type of impact it will surely have on our kids--how they interact, the decisions they make based on online influences, the way they handle solving problems, how their brains are developed after so much online engagement, etc. I personally think our kids are drowning in information but starving for wisdom, direction and guidance. The anxiety and mental illness that can stem from social media is going to be real. We need to teach our kids how to survive in real life, not online. We must teach our kids how to interact and how to be curious, kind, open to listening to others. I see kids now who are so focused on looking at their phones while someone is talking that they cannot even follow a conversation. We must insist as parents that our kids put their phones away and actually talk with people. We need to teach them to listen to different opinions without short dismissal and a shrug of the shoulders. Too many of our teens are so self-absorbed that they don't realize the importance of being connected--to a family, to friends, to peers, to mentors, to the world! The art of good communication needs to make a comeback!

Worth repeating: We have to refrain from letting our kids hate online or else we will never be a civilized country. I hope it's not too late!

How will our kids handle face to face meetings where a supervisor asks for problem solving solutions? How will our kids handle conflict amongst peers in the workforce? Are we equipping our kids with life skills to successfully interact with others? Are they so consumed with having "perfection in life via Instagram" that they cannot face the truth that nothing is perfect? Social media drives kids to compete online for a perfect life. They compare photos and have to snapchat their every single waking moment to their friends. Is this setting them up for big disappointments later? Are we really sure they understand that the world doesn't work only online? We need to have a wake up call on this! It's not reality. These kids need to get jobs where they have bosses and cannot be on their phones 24/7 taking vanity photos of themselves. If we don't get them off these phones, I fear these kids will have problems. Problems with self-esteem, problems with anxiety, problems feeling left out, and problems with interpersonal relationships that will hinder them in life. I feel like this is probable and I hope someone really a lot smarter than me can write about it and help us all figure out how to balance it for our kids.

Here are my tips to parents with teens who are engaging online:

- Set rules for how long they are using their phones: this will work some until they start driving but at least you are suggesting that there should be limits--they understand at some level that too much of the internet can be a bad thing. How can they be getting a good night's sleep when you see they posted something on Instagram at 2:00 a.m.? Watch what time of day or night they post as well as what they post;
- Research is beginning to produce information about teens and social media use. Look it up and see if your child is at risk of some of the pitfalls;
- Teach them what to post and not post: it goes back to Chapter 1 on values: If they value respecting others, they won't post hateful comments, etc.
- Steer away from negativity: this is perhaps the best advice I can give you and there is too much negative and hate online: Tell your kids to steer clear of it and ignore it;
- Pick your weapon: You cannot use every social media channel: Help your kids understand there are different tools for different uses: For example, I use Twitter a lot for news, Facebook for keeping up with friends and family, etc.
- Understand legal risks your kids expose you to when they post: much has been written on this topic so read it and tell your kids that they could get you into a lawsuit by posting things they shouldn't.
- Teach your kids to balance -- there are times to post and times to remain private; Kids today seem to "live life online" for everyone to see;

- Don't let your kids video or tape other kids when something bad is happening like a fight, etc. If they do video it for safety reasons, don't let them post it online--anywhere
- Once something is posted, tell your kids that it is there forever and it's 3 things: 1. Global 2. Permanent 3. Discoverable--as in a court of law--their "digital footprint" starts early.

CHAPTER 8

Common Sense Isn't Common

"The three great essentials to achieve anything worthwhile are: Hard work, Stick-to-itiveness and Common Sense."
--THOMAS A. EDISON

We support the idea of using your head as well as your heart when parenting kids. The problem with it all is that "common sense" is not so common these days. To be good at it, you have to understand what common sense means, right?

Merriam-Webster defines common sense as "good sense and sound judgment in practical matters; synonymous with prudence, level-headedness, discernment, shrewdness, wisdom, perception and the list goes on. One thing I learned from reading Dr. Jensen's book, "The Teenage Brain," is that the ability to discern and make good judgments is not developed until the age of 25--real science behind that statement.

Having a level head when raising kids is one of the best attributes any parent can possess. Too much emotion can lead to a loss of common sense and result in bad parenting choices. It also is very helpful when schools govern applying common sense principles. If kids get the level heads both at school and home, chances are they are ahead of the game by having examples set to learn from.

I have always said, "give me a kid with average grades and common sense, and that kid will be a leader someday." The reality is that we must as parents instill in our kids the ability to discern right from wrong, perceive good from evil and function in a real way in a growing complex, global world. Without common sense, most people are lost.

How do we teach "common sense?" Can it be learned? I think some of it can but I think it has to start with parents who have it and mainly who **practice** it. Our kids are often confused by parents who say "do what I say" but then they don't do it themselves. Kids learn by example and that is something parents need to know right out of the baby gate. If you tell your kids to make up their beds but you don't do that yourself? What does this say? It says that you don't value having a made up bed so why should they? Actions are louder than words. And, when the teenage brain cannot discern what is right or wrong, if they have practiced it, they have a better chance of choosing well. Repeating good choices might make the difference between life and death later.

My parents always said "lead by example." That was a phrase that we heard time and again growing up. And they did practice what they preached. Kids mirror who their parents are so we must start early and apply good, common sense when parenting. I don't think that--as a society--we think about common sense enough. I wish there were classes on it because I think kids need to think about it more. I think common sense applied across the board in all classes in school would be brilliant! One idea I have always supported (but schools have never implemented) is a later start time for high schools and creative solutions for allowing teens to sleep more. Studies and research show that teens are sleep deprived. Their brains are still in development in high school and I have always said that schools would be smart to start a bit later and/or have a study hall as a first period option to allow kids to catch up on homework they may have missed. Teens need more sleep!

School Nights, Sleepovers and Bonfires:
If you have kids, you will be faced with activities on "school nights" and all kinds of parents who have little or no regard for schedules. When the kids were little, I was a "no tolerance for anything on school nights" type of mom. As I got older, and my second one came along, some of that relaxed a bit--not totally. We think kids need sleep and so we had a rule in our house that we avoided late activities on school nights. We couldn't always avoid sporting events (baseball) but by and large, our elementary school aged kids were in bed on time. I think bedtime was around 8:30 but became later when they hit middle school. To me this was just common sense. Unfortunately, not everybody has it!

As kids hit about middle school, sleepovers become the thing and boy did we have them. We had camp outs, sleep overs, pizza parties and more--on weekends. Our daughter also went to them at other people's houses as well. Our house, however, was a magnet for them. Most of them happened around middle school but high school as well--mainly with our daughter. I think girls tend to have them more than boys. Girls like to huddle up in one room, popcorn, junk food, their phones and movies. I was always amazed at how many long-legged teen girls could fit into one bed or on a sofa.

One thing I will say to parents is this: If your kid goes to a sleepover and is not of driving age and has to be picked up, please have the consideration and common sense to pick up your child earlier the next day rather than later. It irritated me no end when our daughter would have friends over and their parents decided to use it as a babysitting service. I learned to start telling parents that all kids needed to be picked up by 10 a.m. (you've already feed them dinner, snacks and breakfast and you don't want to feed them lunch). Don't take advantage of other parents' hospitality, and communicate these expectations to your own kids. My daughter learned fast what kids could and could not come over.

Also, kids who come to my house and don't mind me or accept my rules, are not invited back. We didn't have too much of this, but if you have kids, you'll see some of it. Our daughter had a friend who stayed with us and wouldn't eat much of anything I had prepared. The next morning, she overflowed the toilet upstairs somehow and flooded the bathroom. Some kids are just accidents waiting to happen because they have little common sense. Needless to say, our kids learned who they could invite over and who they could not.

As I have said, we live out from the city some (but close to the schools our kids attended) and on 4 acres with a lake (it's actually like a large farm pond, about 6 acres). When our son was in high school, our house was often the place the boys would congregate to eat, fish, shoot snakes and have bonfires down by the lake. Once they were driving, it was not uncommon for me to come home to 6 trucks in my driveway and in front of my house. Our rule was "no drinking" at the bonfire (but if--for some reason--you are, give us your keys and stay put). We didn't condone drinking but when you have that many kids at your house, somebody is bound to have a cooler in the truck. Amazing how that beer magically appears. Well, I'd rather my kids and their friends be at my house, around a bonfire, talking (and sneaking beer) than in some field and driving home or worse--somewhere else. We have no replacement kids! Thankfully, as I write this, our boys are all over 21 now and we don't have to worry as much about the drinking age. We do, however, still insist on the no drinking and driving. I have plenty of beds, sofas, pillows and blankets. And we love to cook a great, big bacon and egg breakfast for our kids.

Parents who let their kids have big parties at their homes (likely where drugs and alcohol are available) are not parenting. I am against parents who host such parties and we've seen it a few times. Recently our daughter told us about a big party that she went to where the parents were actually there and all the kids were drinking (underage). I told her I was flat against it and also told her of the legal liability those parents must have been oblivious to and that what if some of those kids got hurt or worse--died in a car accident leaving that party. Thankfully Abby agreed and did not stay long at that party. Our rule has always been that if kids are drinking (whether you see it or suspect it) they have to give us the keys and sleep at our house. Or, they can call their parents. It is just not worth it. Be the parent, not the pal. And know your own kids and who they hang out with. If you trust them to do the right things and they have your values, they will likely do the right things.

Here are some common sense parenting tips from my experience that may help young parents:

- Say no more: as parents you will be pulled in a lot of directions and you must do what is right for your family
- Don't let your kids go outside if there is lightning during a rainstorm
- Don't let your kids eat if they are alone: choking is a hazard
- Seek other parents that share your passion for common sense
- Parents who have bad ideas for kids usually don't have much common sense
- Kids need sleep and society will try and tell you they don't: know your child's sleep needs and do everything you can to protect it; science has proven that stress and sleep deprivation can alter brain

development; phones and technology devices can keep kids awake at night when they need to be asleep
- Seek balance in activities for young children and don't over-program them
- Seek schools that embrace common sense teaching and don't overload kids with non-essential work
- Common sense is often your gut or intuition telling you something: listen to it
- Find practical tips from your pediatrician office and read what other mothers and fathers are saying about routines and what works
- Look to older parents who have "been there done that" who have great kids and talk to them about what they did about certain issues
- Common sense says one sport at a time per child: resist the temptation to overload
- Don't buy everything you see--most of the stuff is non-essential: sometimes it can be overwhelming and new parents think they need it all--you don't
- Talk with your kids about common sense and what it means: use examples and make sure they see how common sense strategies work in your family

CHAPTER 9

Schools: What are we REALLY Teaching our Children

> *"In school we learn that mistakes are bad and we are punished for making them. Yet if you look at the way humans are designed to learn, we learn by making mistakes. We learn to walk by falling down. If we never fell down, we would never walk."*
> --ROBERT T. KIYOSAKI (RICH DAD, POOR DAD)

Today's kids are our future. We must equip them with every advantage possible to thrive in this crazy world. Are our colleges and universities up to the task? Are we--as a society and country--focused on teaching them the fundamentals of reading, writing, science and math? Are we equipping them with what they need to be successful in their future careers? Life? Relationships?

To be honest, I wanted to leave this chapter out for fear of "opening the can of worms" but then that would not be the right thing to do. If we are honest, we must accept the fact that our entire educational system is about as wrecked as it can ever be. I'm not talking about the private school out there graduating all of the supercharged, "great at everything" kids. Today we have many school options for our kids: public, private, home, boarding, optional, charter, special needs....the list goes on. You cannot have an honest conversation about the status of our educational system without being political. I would say it is factual that schools have pushed a largely liberal agenda where bias exists and--as we've seen lately--kids are encouraged by teachers to boycott and protest what they don't like.

Okay, liberal or conservative, there is a difference between right and wrong. You think a business is going to tolerate an employee who decides they don't like a new human resources manager and gets their feelings hurt so they decide to protest and take a day off to prove a point? NO. What example are we setting in our colleges for our kids when we do this? Professors are supposed to be grown ups. In our book, **"Students in High Gear,"** we applaud and support those in academia who push an agenda that is high gear in achievement of student goals. You can't be successful if you are worried about hurt feelings and crying spaces. The real world of business employers wants students who can get the job done in spite of what others say, think or do.

Instead of teaching our kids social issues in college (my son actually took a class on LGBT recently) or issues on sexuality....we need to get back to the fundamentals of STEM and STEAM. Science, Technology, Engineering, Arts and Math.

I have already addressed some of the school issues in the early years but when our kids are in college, they are more apt to conform to the ideals and teachings of their teachers and peers. Remember, their frontal lobes of their brains are still in full development mode which means they are literally like sponges when they hit college. I think the pendulum has swung way too far--you can be too far right as well as too far left. Get the politics, social agendas and propaganda out of our colleges and universities. **Parents, don't send colleges money who have fundamentally opposing views of your values.**

Recently, a wealthy friend told me that he had suspended his major gift to his alma mater because of it's liberal ways reported heavily in the media. Interested, I pressed on for more, and he elaborated further telling me that colleges have gotten into the business of pushing the liberal agenda to the point of sacrificing kids actually learning in college. WOW! He further stated that his large annual gift to the annual fund was being suspended until the college changes. That's the "power of the purse" and unfortunately the ONLY way to get real change in play.

We need more business people teaching in the classrooms and we certainly don't need colleges who bully students that have differing viewpoints. Today as I write this, conservative kids are being threatened on campuses across the U.S.A. for their views. This is unacceptable and more importantly, UN-AMERICAN. Speaking of America, when did we get so far away from teaching U.S. history and our Constitution?

Parents, it is up to us to vote with our checkbooks and stop funding these institutions where differing and opposing views are disallowed. Never has it been so apparent as America voted for change and Donald Trump in this last election. **Choose your kids' colleges carefully for it is there that they will be influenced.**

CHAPTER 10

High Gear in College

> *"Your time is limited, so don't waste it living someone else's life."*
>
> --STEVE JOBS

Parents, if you want a useful, practical, from the "trenches" guide for your kids on successful college strategies, you should check out our second book, "Students in High Gear," on Amazon published in 2016. It has garnered national attention as a great guide for millennials and all of the press is captured on the website, www.StudentsinHighGear.com. We think it's important here to highlight some of what is in this book from the parenting side. The book is actually more for the students and has a workbook in the back which helps them set goals and define their objectives post-college hopefully while still in college.

As parents, we must equip our kids with as much information as possible in order for them to be successful. As pointed out in the last chapter, students will face adversity on every level--even from the colleges themselves unfortunately. As parents, we must be the rudder and guiding voice to help them through it.

I think some parents may think that their job is mostly over when their kids go off to college. Ha! Wishful thinking and let me tell you from experience that this is not true. In fact, if you read Dr. Jensen's book referenced earlier, you realize how much your kids do not know when they leave the nest! It is a very exciting time for kids (and parents) when they go off to college. Normally and ideally, parents want their kids to make new friends, experience independent living, learn something in hopes that they can apply it to real life later. Unfortunately, the world is a much more complex, complicated mess than it was 35 years ago when we left the nest.

As written in "Students," my college experience began when my parents packed me and my stuff up in a pickup truck and we drove from Mobile, Alabama to Memphis, Tennessee to settle me into a very prestigious and liberal arts school, Rhodes College (only it was Southwestern at Memphis when I started). Now I did not realize (really) the full scope of what the school could offer me at the time, but took full advantage of it as I grew closer to graduation. Looking back, I think it was a great choice but every family must do what is right for them and their situations. I had received a full scholarship to the University of Alabama but had opted to attend Rhodes--where I had to do a work-study, take student loans and eventually pay them off (If I had to make that choice today, I'd select the place where I had the full scholarship).

Many parents worry too much about sending their kids to the best schools (whatever that really means these days). I think things have changed drastically in academia over the past 20 years so I would challenge parents to really understand what type of college or school is best. Adding to that, is the fact that all kids may not be cut out for attending college. We think a college degree is important, but it is certainly not the only path to success. Vocational skills and all types of skilled labor is needed and many of these positions are highly profitable. As our country's infrastructure has crumbled, the really good, stable jobs of the future may very well be in construction.

Many in academia and perhaps in the corporate C-suite may disagree, but I think what matters more is not the college or university your child attends, but the high gear approach he or she takes to a blazing a path to success. And further, I don't think grades and test scores should limit ANY student's path to success. Give me a student with drive, initiative and a moral compass and I'll show you one who will be successful!

Here are my parenting tips for helping with college decisions and parenting tips while they are in college:

- Apply to a lot of colleges and be deliberate about matching kids' skills with possible curriculum. I think in general we may know our kids' aptitudes but as the brain keeps developing into the 20's....we should be open to new discovery for kids
- Don't send them too far away: I think distance is good but not if they cannot easily (within 6 hours drive) come home if they need to. Pressure on college campuses today is probably worse than pressures in the workforce. Kids need a safe haven called home
- Don't hover--give them space and let them fill out their own college applications, etc.
- Read our "student debt" chapter in our book "Students" for complete information on debt and the problems it is creating for our graduates
- Find creative solutions to attend higher education that doesn't break the bank. We know one family attending 2 years free at a community college that will transfer later to the state college

- **Don't sacrifice your retirement for your kid's college experience.**
- Stay engaged with your college kids but let them reach out to you. They need to learn to be independent.
- Make them work and have jobs! We cannot stress the importance of this enough: don't just give them everything. We make our kids work for their "spending money" like gas and what is up with the Taco Bell? I call it "teenage taco bell."
- Be there when they call you at 3:30 A.M. If you get that call (it will scare you almost to death) use every tool in your toolbox to help them through whatever emergency there is. If someone has used drugs or alcohol to the point of being non-responsive tell your kid to call 911. Most kids don't know what to do in this situation and they think the person needs to "sleep it off." Be ready. Know what to do and help your kids do the right thing. An emergency is not the time to talk about why it happened or blame anyone for what is happening. The key is getting them safely through the emergency. Discussion is for later.
- Spoil them: When our son comes home from college--granted he's in the same city--I will cook or take him to dinner, buy him a pair of jeans he needs, etc. We want our kids to balance being independent but also want them to want to be with us.
- Don't drive your kids crazy and don't get so angry that they won't talk to you: College years can be difficult because they have so much freedom without a fully developed frontal lobe. Instead of reacting saying "What in the heck were you thinking?"...take a breath and just listen to them. Let the paint dry and then loop back around and talk about it when they (and you) are not emotional. If they have another adult--mentor, grandparent, uncle, teacher--engage and see if they can help. Our kids need as much positive support as we can give them from many sources

- Love them fiercely! College kids can be annoying: they know it all don't they? It's like we never went to college and were never 20 ourselves. Don't let that get you down. Love them anyway, celebrate this new chapter in their lives and focus on the fact that in many ways, they truly are smarter than we are and their brains can do more faster...they aren't necessarily wiser though.

CHAPTER 11

Choices and Consequences

> *"Attitude is a choice. Happiness is a choice.*
> *Optimism is a choice. Kindness is a choice. Giving*
> *is a choice. Respect is a choice. Whatever choice*
> *you make makes you. Choose wisely."*
> --Roy T. Bennett (The Light in the Heart)

For each choice we make, there is usually a result. There are good choices and there are bad ones. Experience is the best teacher and many of us learn the hard way how to make the good choices because we've made plenty of bad ones. Teens make bad choices sometimes because they do not have full brain development. There is actual science now behind why teens make bad choices. Again, I am referring to the book, "The Teenage Brain" and it helps us a parent to understand why that part of the brain that triggers good judgment is not there quite yet. I have to stop and think of how God really knew what He was doing and how it is true that kids aren't really mature enough to leave home until they are past 18.

But kids don't always make bad choices. They also make many great choices. And we think good choices are cumulative. Good choices are healthy for our kids and as parents we need to be sure we make them as well. Kids often make choices based on what they think is right. Maybe that's good repetition and good values from the foundational years coming out, but we'll take it!

My kids may not be thrilled that I'm writing my 4th book and highlighting them yet again, but I am so proud of the young adults they are becoming (and they'll appreciate it all later). Our son Bryan, 21 (although now I know his frontal lobe of his brain is still developing) has made good choices along his journey. One of the best choices was to actively pursue (safely) shooting guns, hunting and spending time in the great outdoors. For Bryan, it is therapeutic to shoot guns and a great way to meet like-minded people. One of his mentors is a career law enforcement officer--named David-- who he met through a mutual friend on a turkey hunt. Later, David told us that Bryan was like a son he never had. Together they have spent countless hours practicing, training and shooting at the range. Not only is Bryan a skilled shooter, but he gained a mentor for life. The conversations they have are like gold to me. I have often thought that when Bryan didn't want to listen to what we had to say, he would (and does) listen to David. And there have been times when--as a concerned parent--I talk to David myself. It also helps that he is in law enforcement and on a few occasions I have used him as a sounding board for some questions.

Handling weapons requires safety training, knowledge, practice, strict discipline, and awareness of your surroundings. By shooting with David over the past seven years, Bryan has learned this and further, practiced it. Practice of these good habits is important, and by choosing to spend his free time at the gun range, Bryan has put himself on a great path. Good choices are cumulative. As parents, we hope our kids stay on the good path and off the dangerous ones. Hopefully Bryan will one day have a career that involves law enforcement or maybe armed services. If he chooses business, he'll have a hobby for life in his shooting.

Our daughter, Abby also makes good choices. As previously stated, raising girls is a whole different ball game than raising boys. In general (not always) girls are more mature faster and more deliberate about some things. In our case, Abby's homework being done seemed like it was never an issue. Bryan--on the other hand--seemed to always have homework and never had it done. I'm sure many of you are laughing (so am I) but it's true. Girls get it done and seem to be able to prioritize tasks better when they are younger especially school related. Abby has made great choices in friends as well. Consequently, we love her friends and they are also making good choices. When you choose well, you have less drama.

About sex:
Hopefully, they aren't having it. Realistically, they are. I am not going to get into it much here, but to tell parents that every family is different and most don't want to talk about sex. I grew up in a house where you didn't do it and you certainly never talked about doing it. In our own house, we have tried to be more open with our kids and less threatening about it. There are far worse things for kids to do today than sex, but still--we must educate them as to the diseases they can get, teen pregnancy and other consequences from teenage sex. On the positive side of sex, we have also told our kids what the Bible says and that sex should be saved for the person whom you really love and marry. We have told them how serious it is and that it is meant to be sacred, not casual. I mention it here because the subject comes up when it comes to peer pressure and kids who have friends who are having sex. We hope that our kids have listened to us, will think for themselves and will make good decisions about this based on the values we have hopefully helped instill in them.

We must teach our boys (all of them) respect for women and that "no" means "no." We must also teach our kids about birth control and the dangers of unprotected sex. We started talking to ours about both around the ages of 13 or so and we think it is important for parents to be honest with kids about this. If you have a girl and you are uncomfortable about it, I suggest making an appointment with a good OB/GYN and have them help lead that conversation. If they are sexually active (and don't assume for sure that you know) you may want to consider birth control as well as having a discussion about unprotected sex and the consequences.

Now, back to choices....Parents must also make good choices when it comes to parenting. When your driving teen thinks it is okay to stay out past curfew because they "won't be far from home" (how many times I've heard that) you must say no. And kids will give us so many creative reasons for bending the rules that it's actually comical to me to watch their brains shifting to seek ways around the parental barricade! As a parent, you have to keep them from hurting themselves and you have to keep their safety as your absolute number one priority. Bryan didn't give us as much "pushback" about curfews as Abby did (or maybe I just don't remember it).

And as stated already, our rules were a bit stricter for Abby than they are for Bryan. What? "But Mom, that's so unfair!" Call me unfair all you want! Rape and sex trafficking exist! What frightens me most about being a mom of a beautiful teen girl is kidnapping and human trafficking. I don't know if it's that we hear about it more or that it is increasing (probably both) but it can keep me awake at night. So if I'm unfair or biased, I'll admit it and chalk it up to the fact that our son has had weapon training and our daughter has not. I'm all for girls taking self-defense and I think Abby would put up a good fight, but why even put her in that place in the first place. We must do whatever we can to keep our girls safe. Recently Abby was pushing for a later curfew and when I said no to it, she said, "Mom, I'll be 18 next year and off to college and you won't even know when I come in." I paused and said,

"Well you are not 18 yet and you are not in college yet, and I will keep you safe as long as I can." To Abby's credit, that was the end of it.

And parents of girls, I would offer advice to stay away from malls late at night and places where a lot of strangers are (parking lots). Making choices to get home before midnight and making choices to avoid malls are good ones. Teach them the dangers of parking their cars near a van. Ask them to literally look for a van next to their car. If they see a van parked right by their car, tell them not to go to their car. I have heard from police officers that so many girls are taken by men in vans as they try to enter their own cars. We live in a dangerous world and we must educate ourselves and our kids to prevent as much as we can. I think kids--girls especially--need to be taught how to think fast on their feet and to actually practice what they would do in a crisis. Just as you may teach your kids fire safety in the home, we must teach them street safety! And I have already stated that I think girls should take self-defense courses, and later, after 21 carry permit courses. Abby doesn't shoot as much as Bryan does, but she knows how to.

As parents we must also trust our gut. I have made many a last minute decision or choice by trusting my instincts. As mothers and fathers, we are given the gift of paternal instinctive insights for a reason. Use them. One night Abby went to a birthday party (during the winter months) at a hotel near our big mall. The party was for a fellow classmate and I think they were turning 13. I remember Abby was old enough to have a cell phone so that was about right. I remember not loving the idea of dropping her off at a hotel near this mall. I had a creepy feeling even though there were several parents chaperoning it. It was to be a sleepover in the hotel which had an indoor swimming pool. Sure enough, around 11:00 that night we got a phone call from Abby to come pick her up. Bryan was still in high school so he and my husband went to get her. As it turns out, the police were at the hotel and the kids rooms had been ransacked and all phones stolen by someone watching their rooms. Abby thankfully had put her phone in her boot (when Uggs were in style) so they didn't get hers. I think they eventually caught the thugs which were two young men who were not even guests of the hotel but common thieves. So many hotels are unsecured and law enforcement will tell you that hotels are a big factor in sex crimes and human trafficking.

Lesson learned. I should have said "no" to that party in the first place because my intuition was already telling me so. But we aren't perfect! And the teen years are the most difficult because of these exact examples. You are torn between feeling overprotective and letting them go to a party. It can be overwhelming to raise teens in today's crazy world. That's why I am writing this book in hopes that you younger parents out there can gain some insight from our mistakes, experiences and successes!

Making good choices is also habit forming. I learned in the book "The Teenage Brain" (I know I keep referring to it but it is so good and helpful) that if teens can't scientifically quite make the right decision (like in a split second when something happens and they have to) they will rely on habit. They will end up making the right choice or decision because they have been practicing them and making good ones. That makes such sense to me! So not only are good choices cumulative but they can be habit-forming and thus, life saving. Teens are confronted with more danger than ever and sometimes a choice can mean life or death. Example: your teen daughter decides on a whim not to get into a car with a strange boy much older than her (who may or may not be on drugs). That "little voice" inside her head may not be her brain talking, but yours! Good choices!

Talk with your kids about choices. Help them understand that they have them and sometimes the harder they are to make, the more important they are. And use mistakes--ones both you and they have made--as teaching opportunities not to talk about the "bad thing they did" to make them feel bad, but the consequences of that choice and what could have happened. Talk to them about your bad choices--tell them stories of your own teen years and things that happened. Kids need to hear this and by sharing your stories as a parent, you are reminding them that you have been there too.

So many teens are killed in car accidents and as parents, maybe if we stand firm and make them honor their curfew, we can potentially save lives. As parents, we have a choice: let them talk us into staying out later than they should OR don't. It's often our choices as parents that help these kids through some of hard times. Remember what that dad told me, "we're like pinball flappers bouncing those balls away from those holes."

CHAPTER 12

Accountability

> *"Accountability breeds responsibility."*
> --STEPHEN R. COVEY

One of the qualities I looked for when hiring young people for my PR firm was accountability. Does this person hold herself accountable for her work? Is this person dependable? Will this person be someone we can trust to get the job done? You see there is a direct relationship between good kids and their ability to get good jobs later. As parents, we must teach our kids how to be accountable to themselves, to us and to others. Relationships built on trust are usually ones in which one or more are accountable to one another. In a nutshell, accountability means holding yourself responsible for your actions and that which you can control. To be accountable to someone else means you must respect and respond to them, be responsible in working with them and communicate proactively.

I think kids today who have difficulty sticking to a job or staying in school may never have had to be accountable. As parents, if we don't make our kids accountable for their actions, choices, etc., we are setting them up for failure later in life. Kids who are not accountable usually get into big trouble and end up at dead ends--jail, dead, drugs, etc. Accountability is mandatory if you are my kid (or my employee). It is something we assume our kids will have but we don't talk much about it. I think as parents--especially of teens--we need to talk more about it and use creative examples.

Teens live in such a dynamic, data driven and visual world. They have so many tech toys and so many cool, shiny ways to communicate. It's hard to have a mundane conversation with your teen. To get their attention and hold it, it's like you have to do a "Ted Talk" or something inspiring. OR...you can take away the car keys or cell phone. That certainly gets attention.

Kids need to also know that they need to be accountable to others: classmates when doing projects, teammates in sports, friendships. But it also helps when teens start driving to have them get a job after school or on weekends and in the summer (especially). The value of a job is that your teen has a boss--someone besides you, or his teacher or coach. The boss at the job doesn't care about your teen's love life, home life or any other issue but getting the work done. I think teens who hold jobs while in school become more accountable adults and therefore more reliable employees.

Accountability isn't negative. In fact, it is positive. And, it is a two-way street. Being accountable for each other is a good thing and can foster great relationships in marriages and families later. Just as we hold our kids accountable, they also hold us parents accountable.

I think as a culture, we have lost some of this accountability as young people don't want to be accountable and don't particularly feel accountable. This is not a good thing. You hear about the millennials who don't want full-time jobs because they want to have free time to do what they want. I'm not sure if this is really happening in big numbers, but I do know I have encountered some of it personally. I interviewed a young lady a few years ago who applied for a full-time position with my firm. During the interview, she asked me if it would be possible to work only on Mondays, Wednesdays and Fridays due to a yoga class and some free time she needed. Flabbergasted, I ended the interview and wished her good luck with that! To be accountable to your employer means you work to earn that paycheck and get the job done!

What are colleges saying about "accountability" when they let students skip a class or test so they can go out in the street and protest something they are against? If we teach our kids (either as parents, teachers or coaches) that is is ok to quit something because you don't like it...we are not teaching them accountability.

CHAPTER 13

Grandparents: Standing in the Gap

*"I am little, my legs are short so slow down
a bit while we walk together,
I am little, my ears are new so speak
carefully until they are broken in,
I am little, but my eyes see everything, so allow me to catch
a glimpse of God in your life...then, when you leave someday,
I will not be afraid because I met God when I was with you...
I am little, my feelings are tender so encourage me when
you can. Be patient with all my questions. Someday
you will ask me questions over and over too.
I am little and my hands are small so don't expect
perfection when I play the piano or drop the ball...
I am little but Jesus said people should be just like me.
I dream a lot and I believe your promises. I delight in
others and get hurt over feelings in no time at all...
I am little, so I stand on tiptoe a lot. Give me a
boost and we will both see more together.
I am little, like a special gift from God. Treat me as
precious treasure and both of us increase in wealth...*

> *I am little, so hold me accountable when I goof up, help me with guidance as I grow up, have me disciplined if I act up, herald me with good news so I can catch up and hug me a lot when I give up, especially when I'm scared. Yes, I am little, just like you."*
> -- "I AM LITTLE," BY DR. JOE B. DONAHO (JANUARY, 2000)

I saved the best chapter for the last! The above poem was written by my Dad when our kids were little. It was shared widely around the church where he was a senior pastor at the time he wrote it (Eastminster Presbyterian Church in Columbia, SC where Bryan was baptized). We just love it and I think it is the perfect way to start this chapter.

I'm not a grandparent yet (thank God) but my parents are still with us and have been active and present in meaningful ways in the lives of our kids. Jim's parents--now gone--were when they were very young as well. We are lucky that our kids have known their grandparents who are great reinforcements for us parents when it comes to raising good kids. Through the years we have gone on trips with my parents to the beach, to the TN River, to Fairhope, AL and more with our kids. These trips were not really about the destination itself but the amount of quality time our kids spent with our parents. It's during these large blocks of time that yields great opportunity for growth. I will also say that my dad was instrumental in teaching my husband and son how to deer hunt and saltwater fish. The passion for deer hunting was fueled by the desire to be in the woods at sunrise when the woods 'wake up'--the beauty of the outdoors and the camaraderie they all share when hunting. The hunt is followed by field dressing of any deer killed, a big breakfast at the deer camp and a stop by the processor on the way home. Many a good conversation and stories have been had in deer camps from Texas to Alabama to Tennessee.

Grandparents possess the hindsight and experience that lets them be a calming yet influential force on our kids. When they may not listen to me (especially when they were younger) they may listen to my parents. I know for a fact that our kids asked my parents questions to see (I believe) if they reacted or answered the same way we would. Those are good tests for kids and assuring to our own kids that we aren't crazy. As my parents share the same value system, they are easy relationships without stress and drama. I know not all families are as fortunate as ours and I thank the good Lord for my upbringing and my own parents work shaping me up enough to have children of my own and do a decent job myself!

As parents, you look at how your parents raised you and you make some changes. For example, both of our parents were pretty strict and I think in the 60's everyone pretty much was. We decided not to be quite as strict while still holding to the same values. So you take what you know and then as parents, you apply it to what is right for you and your family. One simple example is that when we were young and lived in Austin, Texas, my mom would not tolerate dirt in the house--AT ALL. We feared the day when we tracked mud in (heaven forbid) on her kitchen floor. She had a temper and we saw it when there was mud or dirt on her clean floor. My dad even built us a "playhouse" in the backyard complete with heat and electricity so we would stay out there and not be in the house so much. No offense to my mom, but if I had a meltdown after each time any one of 5 boys came parading through my house--mud and all--I'd be in a mental institution. See, my mom never had boys. You adapt to what you get and you learn by taking what you know and applying it to parenting your own children. And every child is different.

Grandparents are great when raising children for lots of reasons:

- They can help babysit when you need them
- They can reinforce your values
- Your kids will tell them things they may not tell you or need help with
- They cherish time with their grandchildren and the kids sense it
- They are great teachers and often more patient than parents are
- They have lots of wisdom to impart
- They can spoil your kids without ruining them
- They are positive influences on kids
- They can help financially (in some cases)

I asked my Dad to write the following for this chapter. Here's what he has to say....

"The influence of grandparents on grandchildren is one of the most powerful resources in today's world. Unfortunately our contemporary world leaves many children without the valuable support an extended family can provide. The fragmentation of the American family means many children may never have the benefit of knowing grandparents. This is a reality every child psychologist can appreciate as it removes one of the most obvious resources from the experience of a child growing up with an older adult.

There are many helpful ways to expose a child to a grandparent who is deceased, or lives in a remote location. Photographs, video, Facebook, telling family stories about these grandparents are of great value in giving a child a sense of family even if grandparents are deceased. Hearing these stories of loved ones has a therapeutic benefit in helping a child discover a sense of place in this world. What *a grandparent did in the workforce or accomplished in the war, for example, helps a child know what the family stands for.*

In many families today, grandparents are the primary caregivers left to raise young children. When parents are displaced by death, divorce, prison or geography, many grandparents end up rearing little ones whose families are broken. Fortunate children receive the blessing of mature adults who know the value of a stable environment and educational opportunity.

This relationship between a grandparent and grandchild is powerful and precious for several reasons. First, grandparents see the grandchild in a different light than do mom and dad. For the grandparents, a grandchild is a novelty and not so much a responsibility. Parents have all of the responsibility, the heavy lifting, discipline and correction to be concerned about. They worry about behavioral issues and school work. So always, there is a more stressful atmosphere for parents--even in the best of families.

On the other hand, children see their grandparents in a different light too. To children, grandparents are also a novelty. Grandparents aren't around all the time, don't say 'no' or 'not now' all the time. So what naturally happens is that there is a more relaxed and casual relationship with the grandparents. And grandchildren feel less stress with grandparents who tend not to be the disciplinarians that parents seem to be. Thus, the relationship is frequently rich with opportunity for discussion and fun.

We were vacationing as a family in Point Clear, Alabama with our children and grandchildren. It was summertime and our grandson, Bryan, had brought his casting net down to the beach. The Grand

Hotel where we were staying has a lighted pier where you can fish at night. Bryan was eight years old and as we were walking down to the beach he said suddenly, 'Papa, what time is it?' I looked at my watch and said 'Bryan it's a little after 11:00.' Immediately he stopped and said, 'Papa, is this allowed?' I said, 'what do you mean?' Bryan said, 'I am supposed to be in bed now!' So I laughed and said 'Bryan, when you are fishing with Papa, it's allowed!' And he had the time of his life that night with Papa, totally secure that his new found freedom was allowed. We called it the 'Freedom Boat.'

I give this example to show how time spent with grandparents can shape and reward a growing child. The phenomena of grandchildren and grandparents is curious because those two age groups are really very similar to one another. Grandparents are in their declining years and losing their abilities. Grandchildren, on the other hand, are ascending and gaining in strength. About the place where the two collide they are very similar in outlook and thus they bond with ease.

To reward a child with grandparents is no small thing. And to bless a grandparent with a grandchild is an even greater thing!"
--Dr. Joe B. Donaho

CONCLUSION

If we had to do it all over again.... what would we do differently?

I was talking to Jim about this book and some of the key points and while I was telling him about it what is in it, it occurred to me that maybe we should point out some of the things we didn't do so well. You learn from your mistakes and I think those are great teaching moments, although painful to admit sometimes. Just as no child is perfect, no parent is either. We all make mistakes and every parent will tell you they have made them. So if I had it all to do over again, here are some of the things I would do differently:

Saved more money: I wish I had saved more aggressively. We probably bought a lot of "stuff" we really didn't need and instead we should have saved that money. If you are just starting out as a parent--save early and often.

Made my kids go to church more often: We went to church a lot when the kids were young (and we could make them go). However, as they got older and more independent, we didn't force it. I hope that when they have their own families, they will be back in a church family.

Had less of a temper with them over clean rooms and chores: When you are a young parent, sometimes you can get upset when your kids spew crap (that's the way I like to say it) all over the place. One of my "things" is a clean house: it comes naturally and my mom is the same way. We like a clean house. I wish now--looking back--that I hadn't cared so much about that. I probably had some dandy, head-spinning, meltdowns over their rooms. As the kids have aged, I have become less stressed about it. One day one of my friends saw their rooms and said "Oh wow..doesn't that bother you?" To that I said, "as long as it doesn't come trickling down the stairs, I guess it's okay." Kids are going to have messy rooms. They just are. Don't sweat it. And boys are going to track mud into your clean house. Before you know it they'll be moving out and off to college and you'll have your clean house back. Until then, deal with the muddy boots, clothes everywhere, nail polish stains on the carpet, makeup all over the dresser, a perpetually un-made bed, stickers everywhere, and on and on.

Managed my menopause better: if I'm going to be honest, I didn't manage my mood swings, changing hormones and hot flashes very well. I opted not to go on any drugs or hormone replacement therapy and probably took some of my frustrations out on my husband and kids. I know I did some because after one "incident" where I'm sure tears and yelling--on my part--took place, our son asked Jim: "Dad, can't we just send her somewhere? Like to some spa or something?" We laugh about it now but I am grateful for a patient husband and kids who forgave me for about 2-3 years of that. Menopause is real. I don't regret not taking the drugs but I do regret not finding other ways to handle it. Exercise (which I have done all my life) does help but the other stuff is real. And I went through it early--in my late 40's it started so the kids were unfortunately in the puberty stage--the perfect household hormonal storm, right?

Taken them to get an X-ray when they tell you they broke their arm: Guilty. We let our son go about a week with a "sore arm" until I finally took him in and it was, in fact, fractured. So when our daughter fell at the skating rink on a Saturday night, we went straight to the after hours clinic for that X-ray, and yes, hers was broken as well. We don't race to the doctor every single time something is wrong and if duct tape will do to avoid the ER, we've probably done it. Our kids are both fine, healthy and with boys, it's really a wonder they make it to 18 alive.

Cooked more often: I am cooking now a lot but I wish I had made time to cook more when our kids were younger. I was working so much (and so hard) that I barely had time to pick up something already made to serve. Cooking more means being home more and I wasn't there a lot as a working mom. And sometimes I had dinner meetings with clients and missed the dinner totally. Jim would pick up the slack when needed and that is so important. I don't know how single, working parents do it but they have my complete respect.

Made them both learn how to play a musical instrument well: Bryan took guitar lessons and played an instrument in middle school (because he had to) but I wish both my kids could play the guitar and/or the piano. We didn't force it and maybe we should have. If your kids like music--and show an interest in it--by all means, foster, encourage and provide for that interest.

Made them write more handwritten thank you notes: The art is fading and we need to get it back. I'm for one, guilty of not mandating it. They did it when they were young but not so much anymore in this texting world we live in. Call me old fashioned, but a text is no replacement for a handwritten note.

Did they ever really get into any trouble? If we are going to write a book based on experiences and truth, we have to tell it all. If my kids had really been in bad trouble, I would not be writing this book. I guess that's bad but I wouldn't feel worthy to do it. In fact, to be honest, I worry about "putting it out there" and then having an issue. The thing I had to weigh is risking a "tell it like it is" book in order that I hope my kids stay true to form and out of trouble while helping other parents realize that we must be the parent not the pal to our kids.

This is also a good place to say that some of the wildest and worst kids I ever knew turned out to be fantastic adults (I also knew some who did not). I don't know how, but they did. So there is always hope. For any kid there must be perpetual hope. For the worst kids, we should have hope. We must never give up on our kids. As parents, as schools, as communities and as a society. We must always love our kids--even when they make poor choices.

Okay so did mine ever **really** get into trouble? Not really. Our son did get handcuffed and detained in the back of a squad car by a Barney Fife who thought (incorrectly) he had caught some trespassers. I'll never forget it. We were headed downtown to a fundraiser for cancer patients. This was when Bryan was in high school and was 16 or so. I got a text from him that he was "handcuffed in the back of a squad car for trespassing but all he was doing was trying to fish in a pond" (And don't ask me how he could text in handcuffs but he did). Long story short, he was not the frequent trespasser and had just decided to come fishing with friends on some property he thought looked like a good spot. They let him go but I think scared the crap out of them. It certainly was a good teaching moment on trespassing.

Thankfully (as in on my knees thankful) our kids have never been in serious car accidents like some of their friends have. Part of this is limiting the times of night they can be out and watching out for who they hang out with. The other part is sheer luck and God's protection. One of our non-negotiable rules was no drinking and driving and no riding with kids who had been. We drilled that into their heads when they started driving, and we never stopped drilling. You cannot replace your child or anyone else's for that matter.

Our kids have not been in any serious trouble with the law, they have not done drugs, they have not been harmed, raped, robbed or beat up, nor have they harmed anyone else. We have had some issues with alcohol--not from them but from some of their friends. Nobody has been pregnant or arrested or anything else like that--thank goodness. And it can happen. **EVEN THE MOST WELL INTENTIONED, BEST PARENTS CAN HAVE KIDS WHO GET INTO TROUBLE.** I mean it. We have just been downright lucky and blessed. Yes, our kids are good. But they are not perfect and I go back to Robert Stutman. Keep your kids straight until they are 21 and there's a better than good chance they'll stay that way.

Thank you for reading this and I hope it has been helpful as well as entertaining! Cheers to parenting. And remember: be the parent, not the pal.

Made in the USA
Columbia, SC
22 February 2018